ATLAS OF OUR WORLD

...net ...el of ...em. ...her planets are large balls of dust and rock, or covered with poisonous clouds, the earth is full of life and beauty. The earth looks like a swirly blue marble if you're standing on the moon, but there's so much to see and learn down here. This atlas will take you on a trip around our amazing world of continents, countries, islands, seas, and oceans. You can enjoy the fun facts and activities and you can make this book as colorful as you like.

In Greek mythology Atlas was a Titan who had to bear the weight of the heavens and the earth on his shoulders as a form of punishment. In ancient art he was depicted as a man holding a globe on his back, although the globe actually represented the stars of heaven, not the earth. Back in the 16th century, the first important collection of maps was called an atlas and the name has been used ever since.

Earth as seen from the moon.

Although Greenland is large enough to be a continent, it is considered an island (the largest one on the planet!).

Before the invention of the airplane, people traveled long distances on the oceans. The great explorers were almost always looking for a way to get from one side of the world to the other and many believed there was a Northwest Passage through these islands. Unfortunately, the water between them is covered in ice most of the year.

Several hundred years before Columbus sailed, the Vikings of Scandinavia in northern Europe had already discovered the new world. They built villages in Iceland, Greenland, and Eastern Canada.

NORTH AMERICA

Flag of the United Nations

THE AMERICAS

Exploration of the New World (North, Central, and South America) began in the Bahamas and then spread to the actual continent.

Here's a map of the world as it would have been drawn before Christopher Columbus arrived on the shores of the Americas. Even though Columbus found himself in new lands, he believed that he had sailed to the other side of Asia and that he was in China or Japan.

SOUTH AMERICA

The first circumnavigation (sailing around the globe) of the world was made by the ships commanded by Ferdinand Magellan who found a way around the Americas and into the Pacific ocean, Magellan got as far as the Philippines near Asia before he died, but his ships made it all the way back to Portugal in Europe.

ANTARCTICA

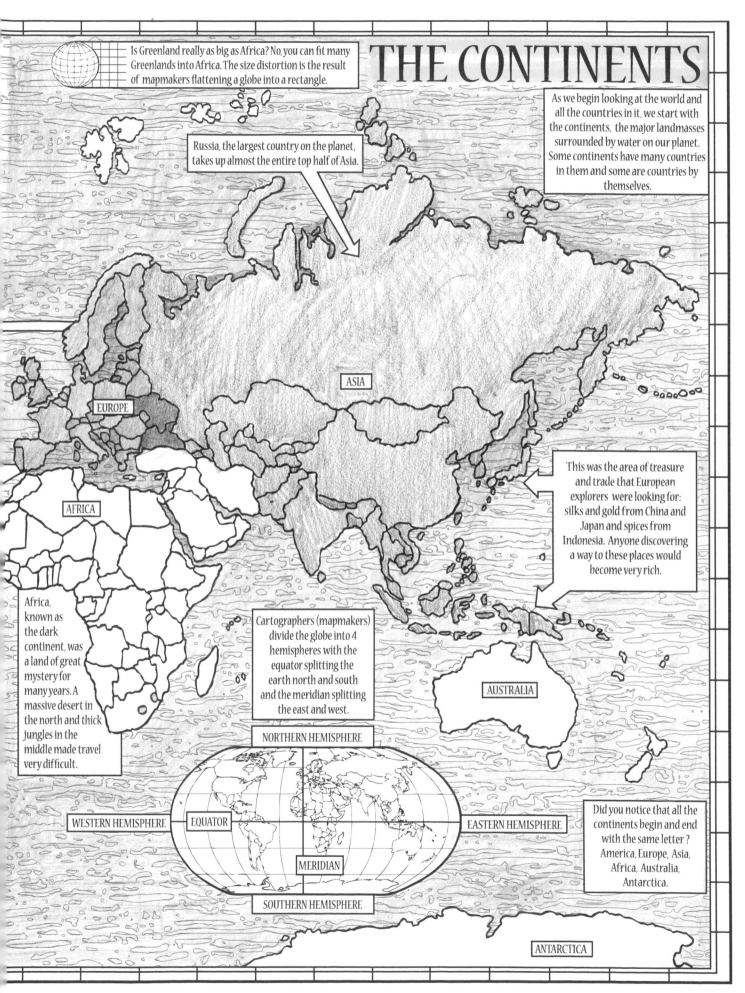

THE CONTINENTS

Is Greenland really as big as Africa? No, you can fit many Greenlands into Africa. The size distortion is the result of mapmakers flattening a globe into a rectangle.

Russia, the largest country on the planet, takes up almost the entire top half of Asia.

As we begin looking at the world and all the countries in it, we start with the continents, the major landmasses surrounded by water on our planet. Some continents have many countries in them and some are countries by themselves.

ASIA

EUROPE

This was the area of treasure and trade that European explorers were looking for: silks and gold from China and Japan and spices from Indonesia. Anyone discovering a way to these places would become very rich.

AFRICA

Africa, known as the dark continent, was a land of great mystery for many years. A massive desert in the north and thick jungles in the middle made travel very difficult.

Cartographers (mapmakers) divide the globe into 4 hemispheres with the equator splitting the earth north and south and the meridian splitting the east and west.

AUSTRALIA

NORTHERN HEMISPHERE

WESTERN HEMISPHERE   EQUATOR

EASTERN HEMISPHERE

MERIDIAN

SOUTHERN HEMISPHERE

Did you notice that all the continents begin and end with the same letter? America, Europe, Asia, Africa, Australia, Antarctica.

ANTARCTICA

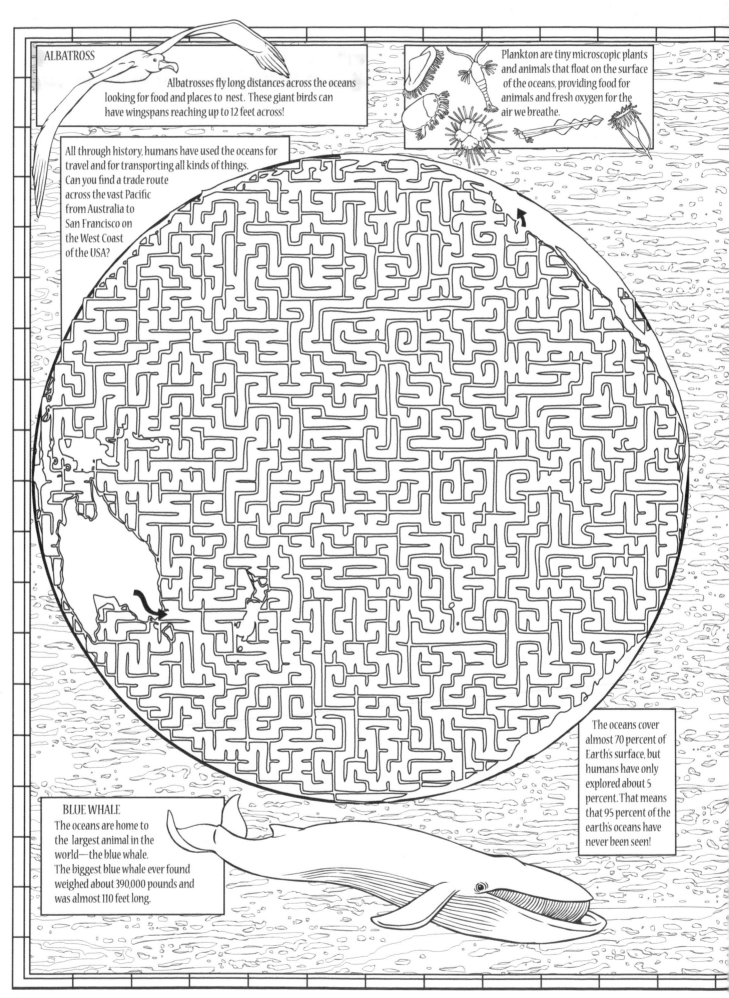

ALBATROSS

Albatrosses fly long distances across the oceans looking for food and places to nest. These giant birds can have wingspans reaching up to 12 feet across!

Plankton are tiny microscopic plants and animals that float on the surface of the oceans, providing food for animals and fresh oxygen for the air we breathe.

All through history, humans have used the oceans for travel and for transporting all kinds of things. Can you find a trade route across the vast Pacific from Australia to San Francisco on the West Coast of the USA?

The oceans cover almost 70 percent of Earth's surface, but humans have only explored about 5 percent. That means that 95 percent of the earth's oceans have never been seen!

BLUE WHALE
The oceans are home to the largest animal in the world—the blue whale. The biggest blue whale ever found weighed about 390,000 pounds and was almost 110 feet long.

THE OCEANS

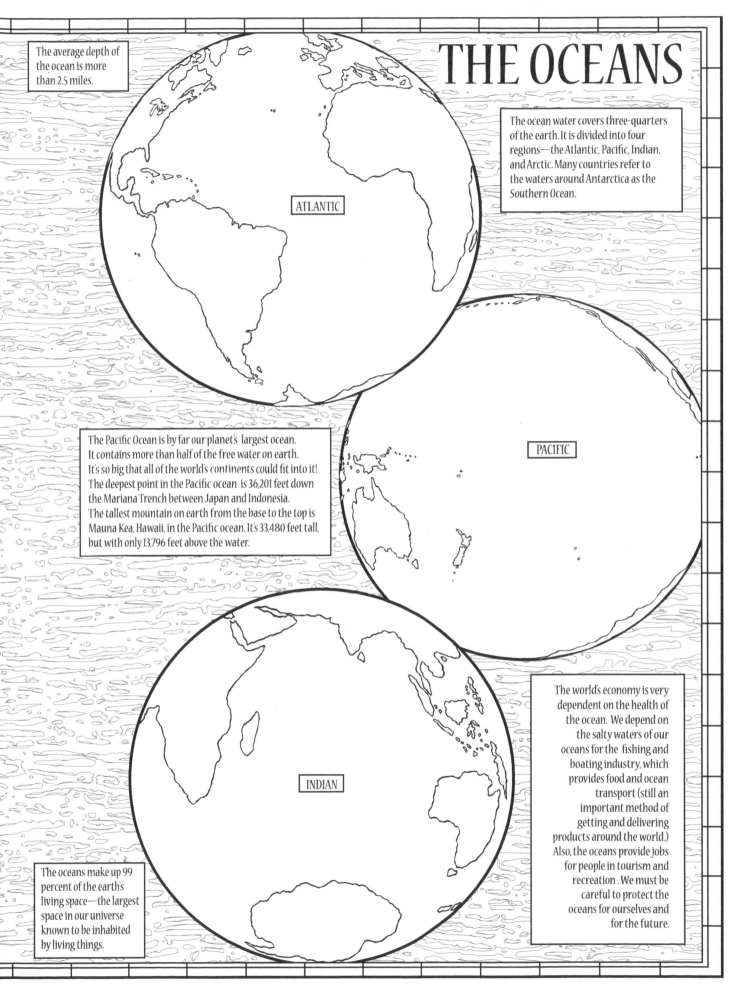

The average depth of the ocean is more than 2.5 miles.

The ocean water covers three-quarters of the earth. It is divided into four regions—the Atlantic, Pacific, Indian, and Arctic. Many countries refer to the waters around Antarctica as the Southern Ocean.

ATLANTIC

The Pacific Ocean is by far our planet's largest ocean. It contains more than half of the free water on earth. It's so big that all of the world's continents could fit into it! The deepest point in the Pacific ocean is 36,201 feet down the Mariana Trench between Japan and Indonesia. The tallest mountain on earth from the base to the top is Mauna Kea, Hawaii, in the Pacific ocean. It's 33,480 feet tall, but with only 13,796 feet above the water.

PACIFIC

INDIAN

The world's economy is very dependent on the health of the ocean. We depend on the salty waters of our oceans for the fishing and boating industry, which provides food and ocean transport (still an important method of getting and delivering products around the world.) Also, the oceans provide jobs for people in tourism and recreation . We must be careful to protect the oceans for ourselves and for the future.

The oceans make up 99 percent of the earth's living space—the largest space in our universe known to be inhabited by living things.

5

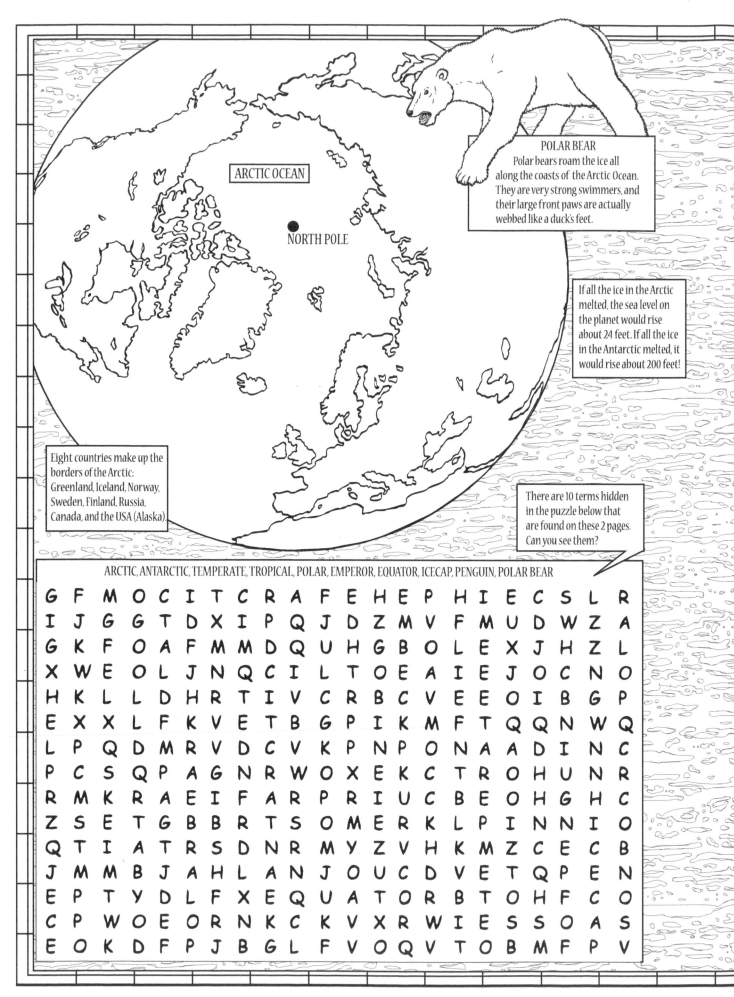

ARCTIC OCEAN

NORTH POLE

POLAR BEAR
Polar bears roam the ice all along the coasts of the Arctic Ocean. They are very strong swimmers, and their large front paws are actually webbed like a duck's feet.

If all the ice in the Arctic melted, the sea level on the planet would rise about 24 feet. If all the ice in the Antarctic melted, it would rise about 200 feet!

Eight countries make up the borders of the Arctic: Greenland, Iceland, Norway, Sweden, Finland, Russia, Canada, and the USA (Alaska).

There are 10 terms hidden in the puzzle below that are found on these 2 pages. Can you see them?

ARCTIC, ANTARCTIC, TEMPERATE, TROPICAL, POLAR, EMPEROR, EQUATOR, ICECAP, PENGUIN, POLAR BEAR

```
G F M O C I T C R A F E H E P H I E C S L R
I J G G T D X I P Q J D Z M V F M U D W Z A
G K F O A F M M D Q U H G B O L E X J H Z L
X W E O L J N Q C I L T O E A I E J O C N O
H K L L D H R T I V C R B C V E E O I B G P
E X X L F K V E T B G P I K M F T Q Q N W Q
L P Q D M R V D C V K P N P O N A A D I N C
P C S Q P A G N R W O X E K C T R O H U N R
R M K R A E I F A R P R I U C B E O H G H C
Z S E T G B B R T S O M E R K L P I N N I O
Q T I A T R S D N R M Y Z V H K M Z C E C B
J M M B J A H L A N J O U C D V E T Q P E N
E P T Y D L F X E Q U A T O R B T O H F C O
C P W O E O R N K C K V X R W I E S S O A S
E O K D F P J B G L F V O Q V T O B M F P V
```

6

NORTH AND SOUTH POLES
(Earth's Top and Bottom)

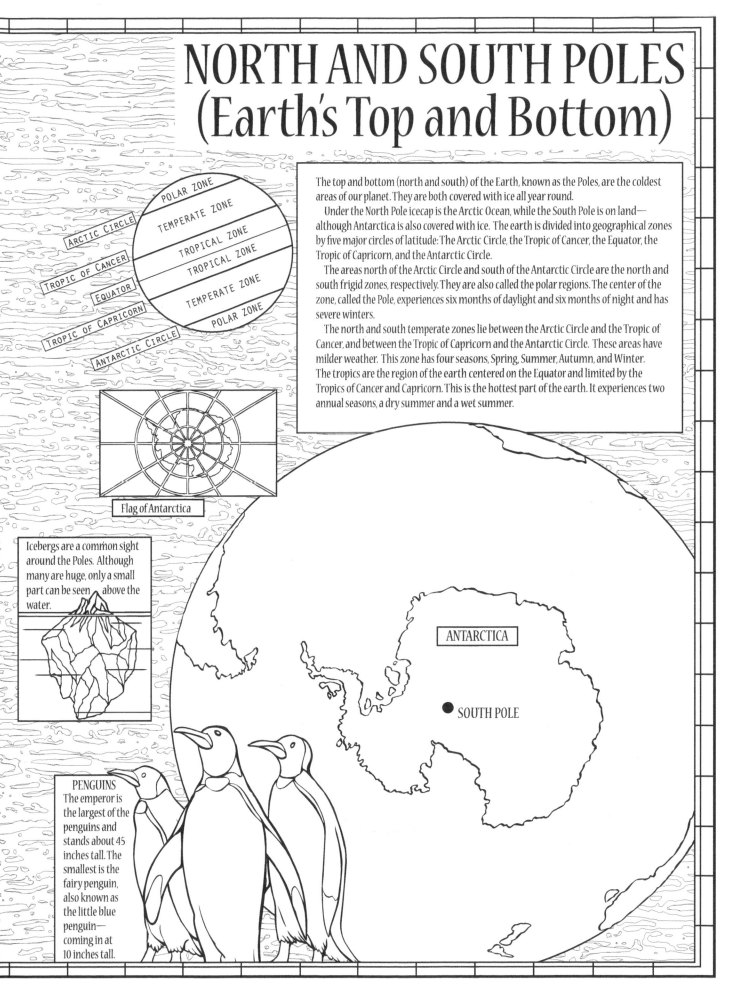

POLAR ZONE

ARCTIC CIRCLE

TEMPERATE ZONE

TROPIC OF CANCER

TROPICAL ZONE

EQUATOR

TROPICAL ZONE

TROPIC OF CAPRICORN

TEMPERATE ZONE

ANTARCTIC CIRCLE

POLAR ZONE

The top and bottom (north and south) of the Earth, known as the Poles, are the coldest areas of our planet. They are both covered with ice all year round.

Under the North Pole icecap is the Arctic Ocean, while the South Pole is on land—although Antarctica is also covered with ice. The earth is divided into geographical zones by five major circles of latitude: The Arctic Circle, the Tropic of Cancer, the Equator, the Tropic of Capricorn, and the Antarctic Circle.

The areas north of the Arctic Circle and south of the Antarctic Circle are the north and south frigid zones, respectively. They are also called the polar regions. The center of the zone, called the Pole, experiences six months of daylight and six months of night and has severe winters.

The north and south temperate zones lie between the Arctic Circle and the Tropic of Cancer, and between the Tropic of Capricorn and the Antarctic Circle. These areas have milder weather. This zone has four seasons, Spring, Summer, Autumn, and Winter. The tropics are the region of the earth centered on the Equator and limited by the Tropics of Cancer and Capricorn. This is the hottest part of the earth. It experiences two annual seasons, a dry summer and a wet summer.

Flag of Antarctica

Icebergs are a common sight around the Poles. Although many are huge, only a small part can be seen above the water.

ANTARCTICA

● SOUTH POLE

PENGUINS
The emperor is the largest of the penguins and stands about 45 inches tall. The smallest is the fairy penguin, also known as the little blue penguin—coming in at 10 inches tall.

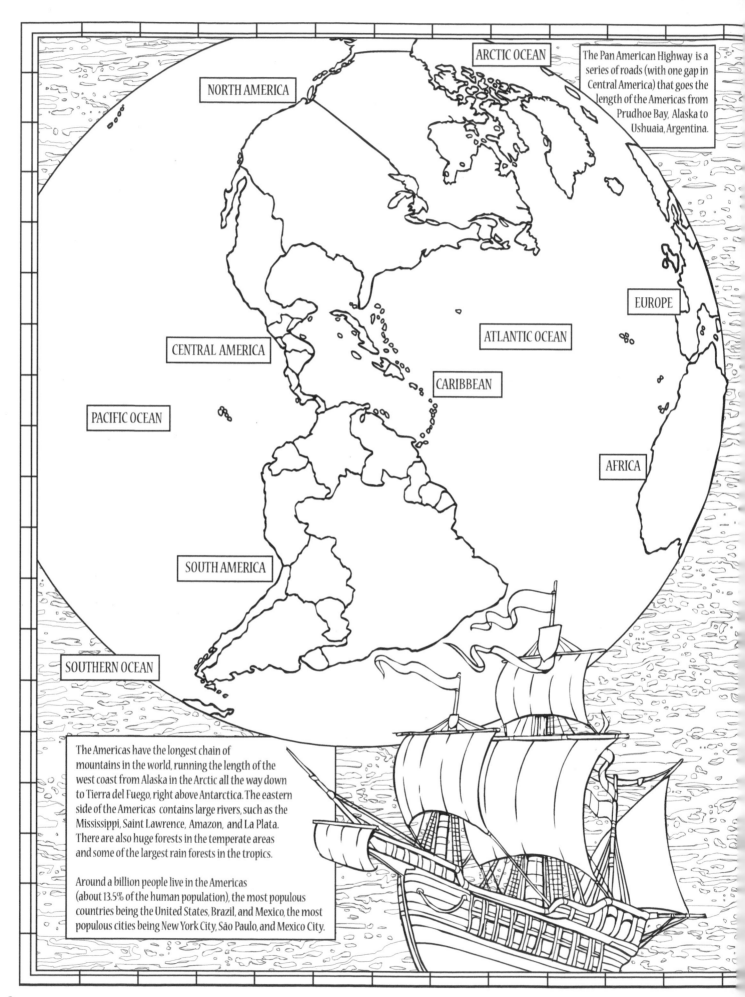

ARCTIC OCEAN

NORTH AMERICA

The Pan American Highway is a series of roads (with one gap in Central America) that goes the length of the Americas from Prudhoe Bay, Alaska to Ushuaia, Argentina.

EUROPE

ATLANTIC OCEAN

CENTRAL AMERICA

CARIBBEAN

PACIFIC OCEAN

AFRICA

SOUTH AMERICA

SOUTHERN OCEAN

The Americas have the longest chain of mountains in the world, running the length of the west coast from Alaska in the Arctic all the way down to Tierra del Fuego, right above Antarctica. The eastern side of the Americas contains large rivers, such as the Mississippi, Saint Lawrence, Amazon, and La Plata. There are also huge forests in the temperate areas and some of the largest rain forests in the tropics.

Around a billion people live in the Americas (about 13.5% of the human population), the most populous countries being the United States, Brazil, and Mexico, the most populous cities being New York City, São Paulo, and Mexico City.

THE AMERICAS
(The Western Hemisphere)

Before the discovery of the Americas, these foods were almost completely unknown to the rest of the world.

POTATOES

AVOCADOS

CHOCOLATE

CORN

TOMATOES

PEPPERS

The "Age of Discovery," from the 15th to the 17th century, changed the world forever. Europeans explored Africa, the Americas, Asia, and the islands of the Pacific ocean seeking trade routes to "the East Indies" (India, China, Japan and the Spice Islands) to trade in gold, silver and spices. It was at this time that the western hemisphere was explored, even though many early explorers (including Columbus) thought they were in Asia.

Amerigo Vespucci was an Italian explorer, navigator, and mapmaker (cartographer) who first showed that the coast of the "New World" was not Asia's eastern coast but instead was an entirely separate land, previously unknown to peoples of Europe, Africa, and Asia. These new continents became known as "America", from Vespucci's first name.

Here's a puzzle using words that are found on these 2 pages. Can you find them by solving the clues below?

The arrival of Europeans during the age of exploration in the 15th and 16th centuries brought the languages that are most used today in the western hemisphere: English, Spanish, Portuguese, and French.

Before the coming of the Europeans the Western Hemisphere had never known diseases like smallpox, typhus, cholera, and measles. Many native peoples became ill and died because they had no immunity.

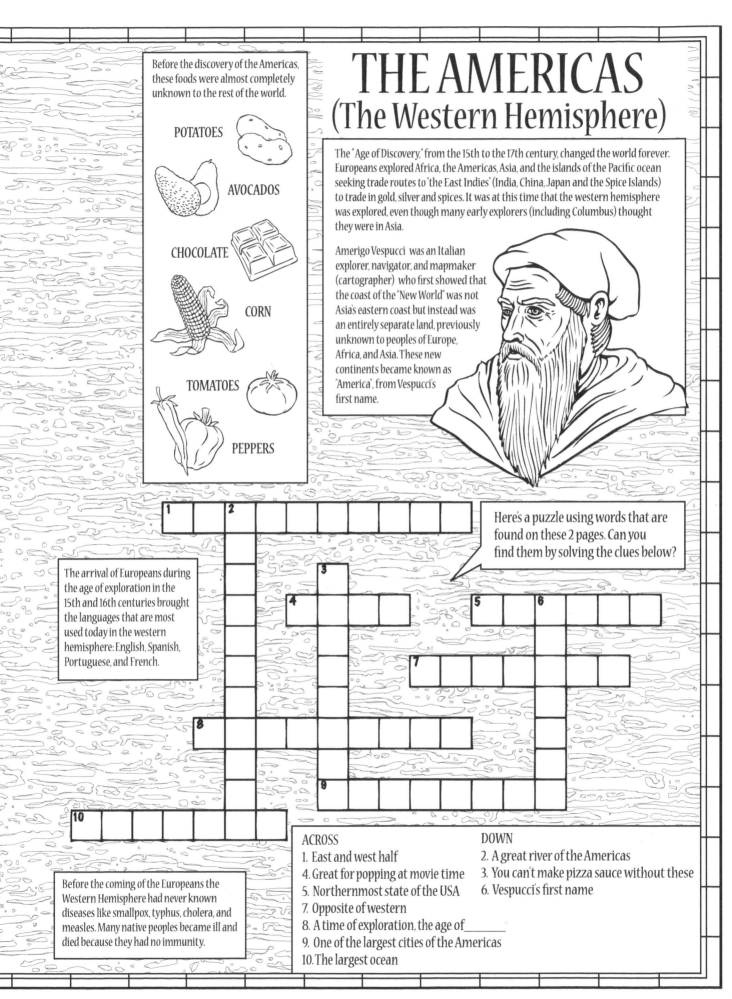

ACROSS
1. East and west half
4. Great for popping at movie time
5. Northernmost state of the USA
7. Opposite of western
8. A time of exploration, the age of_____
9. One of the largest cities of the Americas
10. The largest ocean

DOWN
2. A great river of the Americas
3. You can't make pizza sauce without these
6. Vespucci's first name

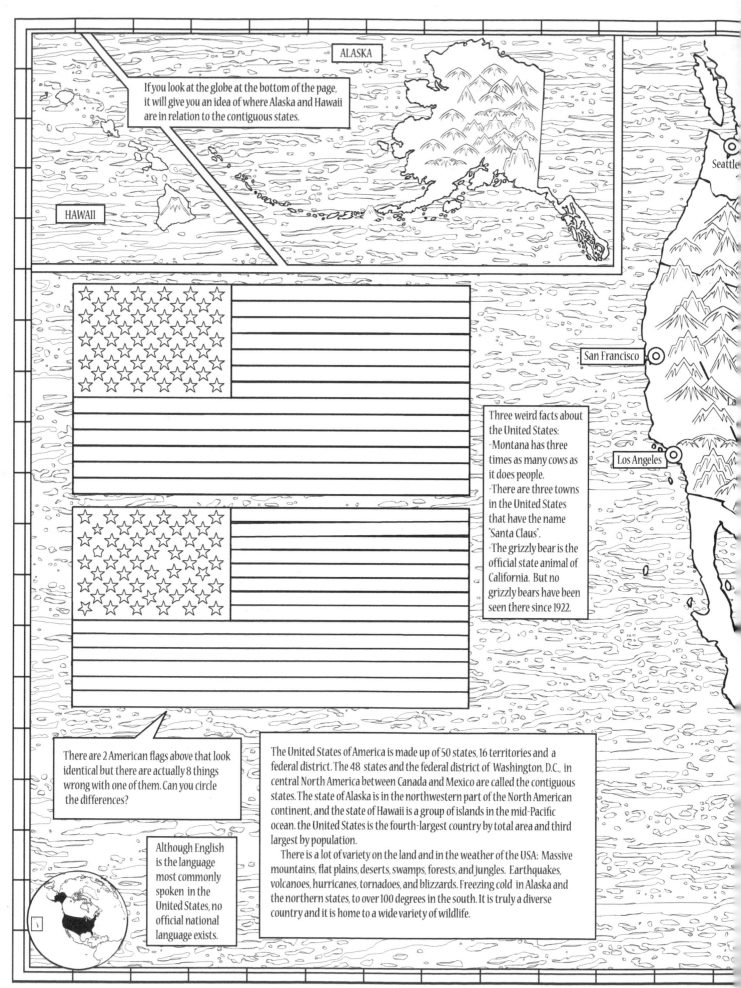

ALASKA

If you look at the globe at the bottom of the page, it will give you an idea of where Alaska and Hawaii are in relation to the contiguous states.

HAWAII

Seattle

San Francisco

Los Angeles

Three weird facts about the United States:
-Montana has three times as many cows as it does people.
-There are three towns in the United States that have the name "Santa Claus".
-The grizzly bear is the official state animal of California. But no grizzly bears have been seen there since 1922.

There are 2 American flags above that look identical but there are actually 8 things wrong with one of them. Can you circle the differences?

Although English is the language most commonly spoken in the United States, no official national language exists.

The United States of America is made up of 50 states, 16 territories and a federal district. The 48 states and the federal district of Washington, D.C., in central North America between Canada and Mexico are called the contiguous states. The state of Alaska is in the northwestern part of the North American continent, and the state of Hawaii is a group of islands in the mid-Pacific ocean. the United States is the fourth-largest country by total area and third largest by population.

There is a lot of variety on the land and in the weather of the USA: Massive mountains, flat plains, deserts, swamps, forests, and jungles. Earthquakes, volcanoes, hurricanes, tornadoes, and blizzards. Freezing cold in Alaska and the northern states, to over 100 degrees in the south. It is truly a diverse country and it is home to a wide variety of wildlife.

THE UNITED STATES OF AMERICA
(and Major Cities)

CANADA

Great Lakes Region

Rocky Mountains

Great Plains

Chicago

New York City

Philadelphia

Appalachian Mountains

Washington D.C.

ATLANTIC OCEAN

Houston

New Orleans

GULF OF MEXICO

Miami

MEXICO

The worst natural disaster in United States history was a hurricane that hit Galveston on the Gulf coast of Texas in 1900. Over 8000 people were killed.

PACIFIC OCEAN

The oldest game in America is stickball, played by the Choctaw Indians of Mississippi.

CARIBBEAN SEA

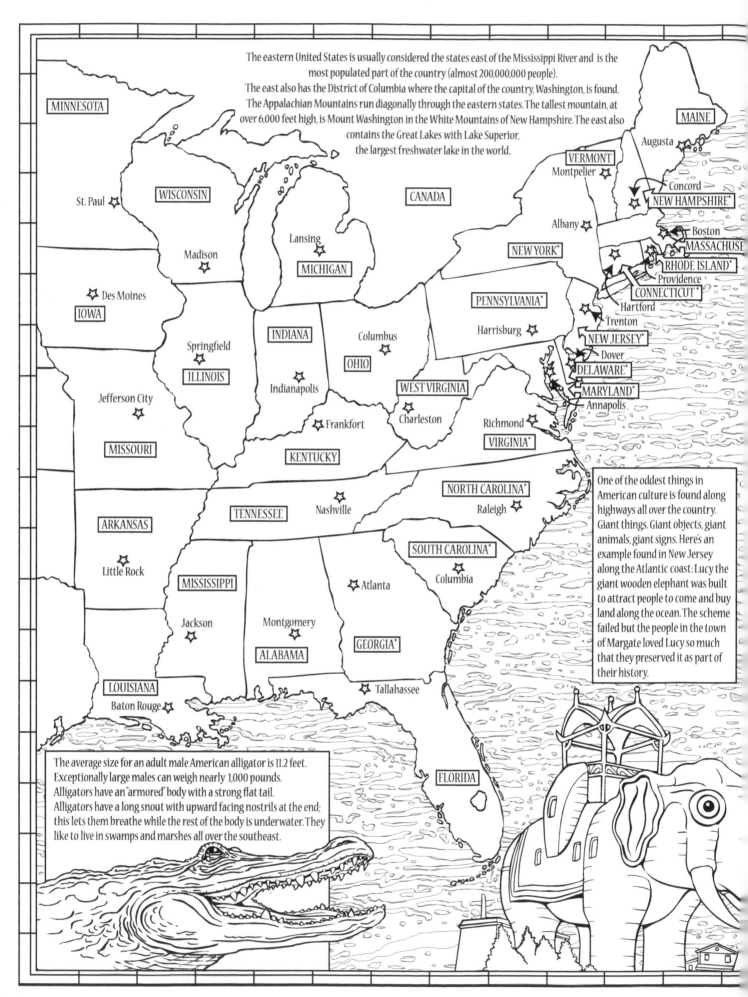

The eastern United States is usually considered the states east of the Mississippi River and is the most populated part of the country (almost 200,000,000 people). The east also has the District of Columbia where the capital of the country, Washington, is found. The Appalachian Mountains run diagonally through the eastern states. The tallest mountain, at over 6,000 feet high, is Mount Washington in the White Mountains of New Hampshire. The east also contains the Great Lakes with Lake Superior, the largest freshwater lake in the world.

MINNESOTA

MAINE

Augusta

VERMONT
Montpelier

Concord
NEW HAMPSHIRE*

St. Paul

WISCONSIN

CANADA

Albany

Boston
MASSACHUSE

Lansing

NEW YORK*

RHODE ISLAND*

Madison

MICHIGAN

Providence
CONNECTICUT*

Des Moines

PENNSYLVANIA*

Hartford

IOWA

INDIANA

Columbus

Harrisburg

Trenton
NEW JERSEY*

Springfield

OHIO

Dover
DELAWARE*

ILLINOIS

Indianapolis

MARYLAND*
Annapolis

Jefferson City

Frankfort

Charleston

Richmond

WEST VIRGINIA

VIRGINIA*

MISSOURI

KENTUCKY

NORTH CAROLINA*
Raleigh

TENNESSEE

Nashville

ARKANSAS

SOUTH CAROLINA*

Little Rock

MISSISSIPPI

Atlanta

Columbia

Jackson

Montgomery

GEORGIA*

ALABAMA

LOUISIANA
Baton Rouge

Tallahassee

One of the oddest things in American culture is found along highways all over the country. Giant things. Giant objects, giant animals, giant signs. Here's an example found in New Jersey along the Atlantic coast: Lucy the giant wooden elephant was built to attract people to come and buy land along the ocean. The scheme failed but the people in the town of Margate loved Lucy so much that they preserved it as part of their history.

FLORIDA

The average size for an adult male American alligator is 11.2 feet. Exceptionally large males can weigh nearly 1,000 pounds. Alligators have an "armored" body with a strong flat tail. Alligators have a long snout with upward facing nostrils at the end; this lets them breathe while the rest of the body is underwater. They like to live in swamps and marshes all over the southeast.

EASTERN UNITED STATES
States and Capitals

The sea was very important to the development of the United States. Trade, transportation and fishing provided jobs and opportunity. For centuries, lighthouse warnings have saved ships and lives along 6,000 miles of Atlantic coastline. Tall and white or short and striped, each lighthouse is different. Mostly abandoned now, they are still symbols of the region and its history of seafaring.

The United States began as 13 states located along the Atlantic coast. These were British colonies that eventually gained independence and became a nation.

The original 13 states on the map have an asterisk* next to them. Find the 13 states on the map and then see if you can find them in this puzzle.

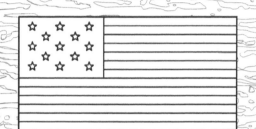

Original American flag with 13 stars

```
B  B  W  H  I  G  R  S  I  P  S  N  F  H  F  L  K  B  F  C  L  O  W  X  H
S  J  J  R  D  C  J  J  D  X  G  J  Y  E  S  R  E  J  W  E  N  M  I  M  R
X  J  Z  W  T  R  Y  V  D  A  F  A  R  O  L  W  V  G  A  N  E  R  M  W  S
B  W  W  Q  N  A  T  G  M  X  B  E  K  N  Q  V  N  H  A  E  E  C  B  D
G  D  Z  N  O  R  T  H  C  A  R  O  L  I  N  A  U  B  B  N  F  A  E  X  Y
H  G  E  O  R  G  I  A  R  B  K  H  Z  S  S  H  H  A  O  D  A  C  A  K  S
T  M  Z  K  E  Y  T  K  J  I  K  H  B  K  I  A  O  U  N  L  I  U  S  Q  V
W  C  X  A  T  H  P  R  M  R  H  O  D  E  I  S  L  A  N  D  C  O  I  K  Q
T  D  I  O  Z  P  F  F  F  K  R  O  Y  W  E  N  M  W  H  O  E  I  S  A  V
N  M  M  Y  U  C  O  T  Q  B  A  H  P  O  E  L  F  N  R  T  O  X  Y  X
D  J  A  A  T  U  C  H  S  N  A  N  H  A  A  Q  C  N  U  Q  M  V  M  S  Q
O  R  Q  F  L  M  A  F  L  M  Q  A  M  H  K  A  E  I  K  O  E  E  E  S  A
V  T  W  J  S  Y  L  T  S  T  T  E  S  U  H  C  A  S  S  A  M  Y  W  O  N
M  F  W  M  O  J  R  O  K  O  N  J  G  N  T  N  E  H  L  E  T  C  P  U  Y
E  R  I  H  S  P  M  A  H  W  E  N  D  I  I  S  L  M  N  T  N  M  D  T  D
P  O  M  Q  R  D  D  G  M  H  O  F  C  H  E  P  D  A  U  Z  S  Q  K  H  P
X  V  Q  V  R  W  K  E  V  L  M  U  C  W  A  V  R  H  I  I  K  J  V  C  W
J  U  B  J  Q  M  V  Z  L  H  T  F  E  P  M  M  N  B  B  N  T  I  R  A  F
I  F  Z  Z  Z  Y  A  P  H  A  V  A  E  M  I  O  G  B  H  C  I  D  A  R  N
A  R  K  J  U  O  H  I  J  D  W  R  D  M  X  V  W  F  H  I  R  G  M  O  I
P  E  N  N  S  Y  L  V  A  N  I  A  V  E  W  A  O  I  K  N  G  B  R  L  Y
D  X  V  X  D  F  Q  J  U  M  A  L  R  Y  W  X  P  G  Q  Z  M  N  V  I  C
V  N  G  B  I  Q  X  B  Q  N  Q  N  U  E  V  T  H  C  N  E  Z  2  H  V
Y  Y  X  T  Q  A  C  K  Z  L  G  U  I  R  H  C  K  L  G  P  T  E  U  A  C
A  V  B  I  N  W  V  T  L  Y  B  X  U  X  I  L  D  E  C  X  I  P  X  G  O
```

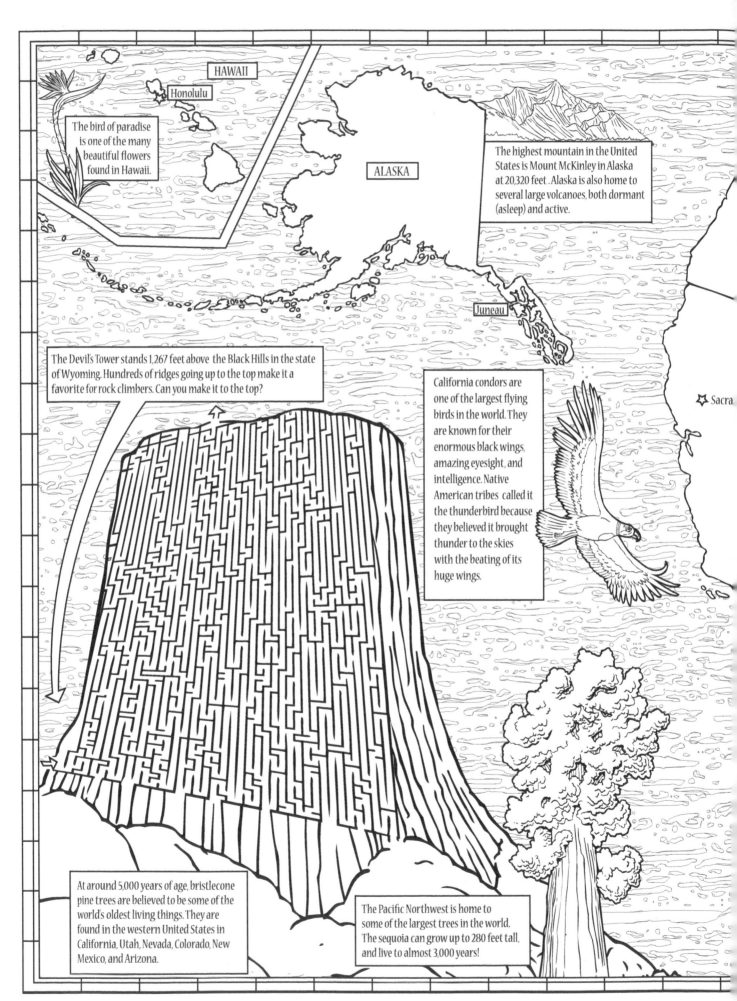

HAWAII

Honolulu

The bird of paradise is one of the many beautiful flowers found in Hawaii.

ALASKA

The highest mountain in the United States is Mount McKinley in Alaska at 20,320 feet. Alaska is also home to several large volcanoes, both dormant (asleep) and active.

Juneau

The Devil's Tower stands 1,267 feet above the Black Hills in the state of Wyoming. Hundreds of ridges going up to the top make it a favorite for rock climbers. Can you make it to the top?

Sacra

California condors are one of the largest flying birds in the world. They are known for their enormous black wings, amazing eyesight, and intelligence. Native American tribes called it the thunderbird because they believed it brought thunder to the skies with the beating of its huge wings.

At around 5,000 years of age, bristlecone pine trees are believed to be some of the world's oldest living things. They are found in the western United States in California, Utah, Nevada, Colorado, New Mexico, and Arizona.

The Pacific Northwest is home to some of the largest trees in the world. The sequoia can grow up to 280 feet tall, and live to almost 3,000 years!

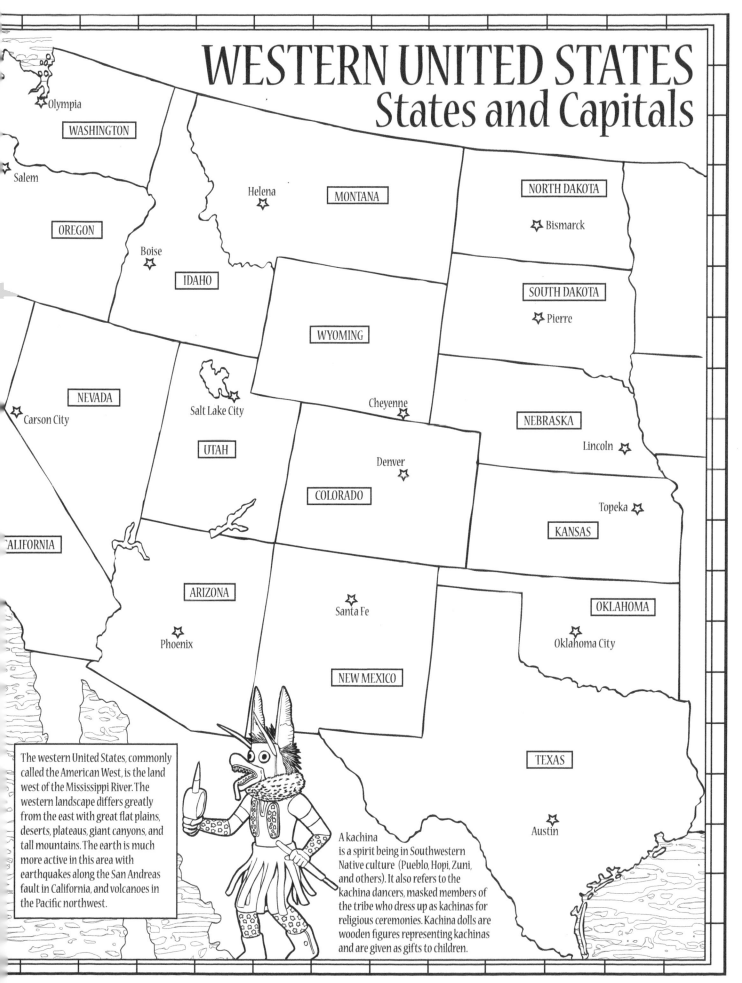

WESTERN UNITED STATES
States and Capitals

Olympia
WASHINGTON

Salem

OREGON

Helena
MONTANA

Boise
IDAHO

NORTH DAKOTA
Bismarck

SOUTH DAKOTA
Pierre

WYOMING

Cheyenne

NEVADA
Carson City

Salt Lake City

NEBRASKA

Lincoln

UTAH

Denver

COLORADO

CALIFORNIA

Topeka

KANSAS

ARIZONA

Santa Fe

Phoenix

NEW MEXICO

OKLAHOMA

Oklahoma City

TEXAS

Austin

The western United States, commonly called the American West, is the land west of the Mississippi River. The western landscape differs greatly from the east with great flat plains, deserts, plateaus, giant canyons, and tall mountains. The earth is much more active in this area with earthquakes along the San Andreas fault in California, and volcanoes in the Pacific northwest.

A kachina is a spirit being in Southwestern Native culture (Pueblo, Hopi, Zuni, and others). It also refers to the kachina dancers, masked members of the tribe who dress up as kachinas for religious ceremonies. Kachina dolls are wooden figures representing kachinas and are given as gifts to children.

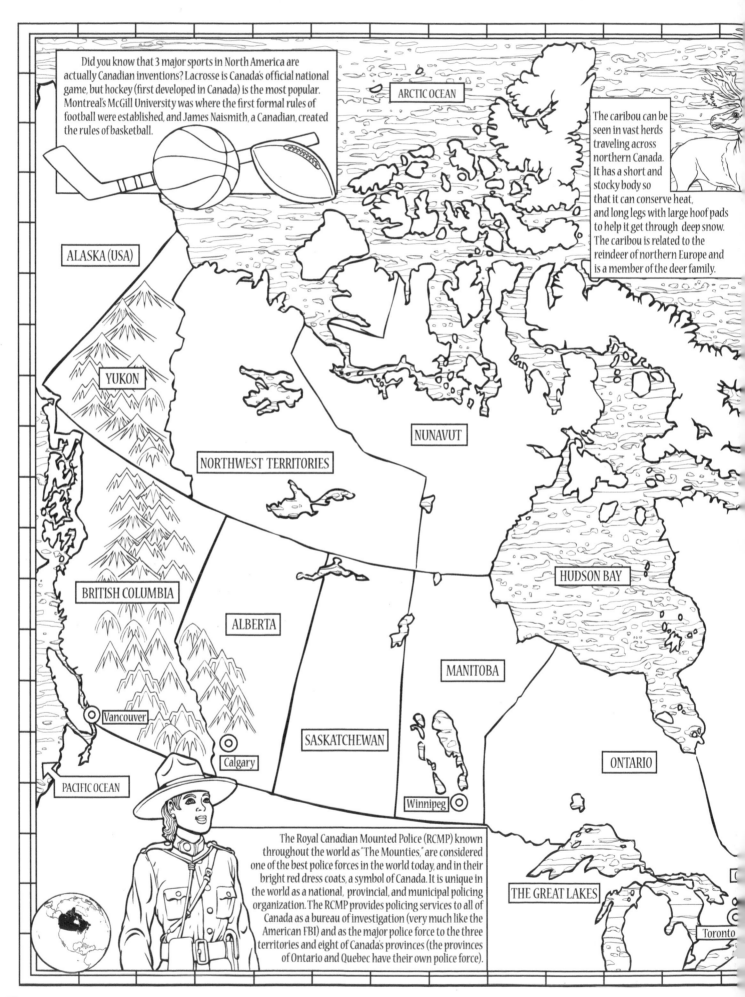

Did you know that 3 major sports in North America are actually Canadian inventions? Lacrosse is Canada's official national game, but hockey (first developed in Canada) is the most popular. Montreal's McGill University was where the first formal rules of football were established, and James Naismith, a Canadian, created the rules of basketball.

ARCTIC OCEAN

The caribou can be seen in vast herds traveling across northern Canada. It has a short and stocky body so that it can conserve heat, and long legs with large hoof pads to help it get through deep snow. The caribou is related to the reindeer of northern Europe and is a member of the deer family.

ALASKA (USA)

YUKON

NORTHWEST TERRITORIES

NUNAVUT

BRITISH COLUMBIA

ALBERTA

MANITOBA

HUDSON BAY

Vancouver

Calgary

SASKATCHEWAN

ONTARIO

PACIFIC OCEAN

Winnipeg

The Royal Canadian Mounted Police (RCMP) known throughout the world as "The Mounties," are considered one of the best police forces in the world today, and in their bright red dress coats, a symbol of Canada. It is unique in the world as a national, provincial, and municipal policing organization. The RCMP provides policing services to all of Canada as a bureau of investigation (very much like the American FBI) and as the major police force to the three territories and eight of Canada's provinces (the provinces of Ontario and Quebec have their own police force).

THE GREAT LAKES

Toronto

CANADA
Provinces and Territories
(and Major Cities)

Canada is the world's second-largest country (Russia is the largest) and consists of 10 provinces and 3 territories. It takes up the whole northern part of the continent (except for the State of Alaska) and is surrounded by 3 oceans, the Atlantic, the Pacific, and the Arctic. Its border with the United States of America is the world's longest land border shared by two countries.

Canada is officially bilingual, meaning that two languages, French and English, are used equally in the government, the workplace, and even on all product packages. Although the Canadian government differs from the American government, both countries are similar in culture and continue to share trade and defense. As countries, they are each other's best friend.

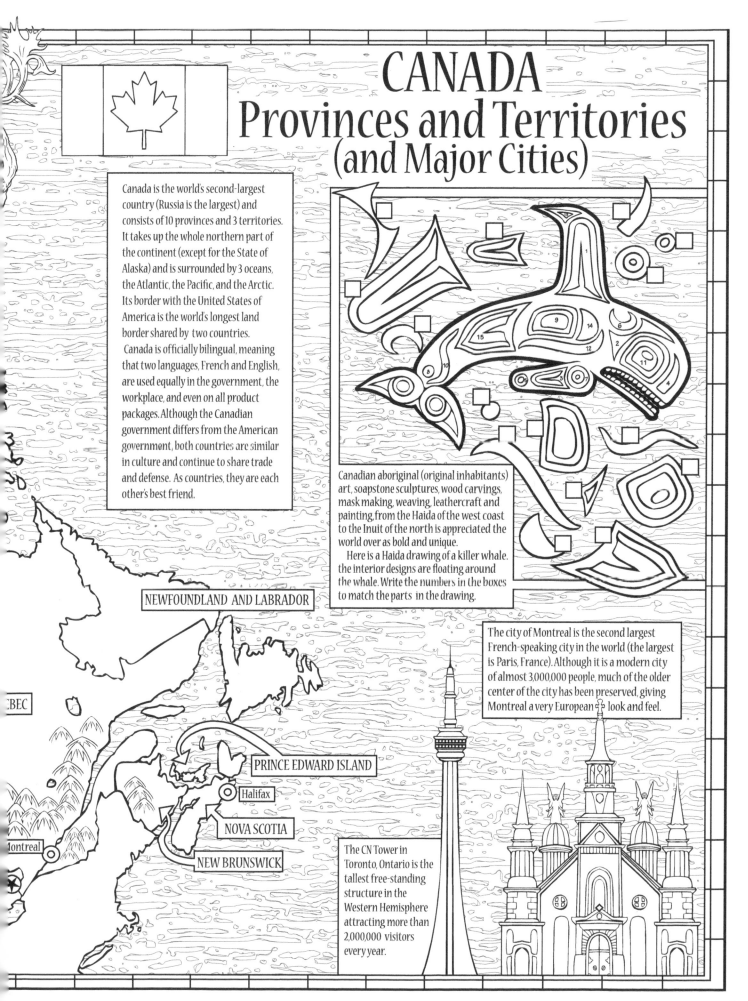

Canadian aboriginal (original inhabitants) art, soapstone sculptures, wood carvings, mask making, weaving, leathercraft and painting, from the Haida of the west coast to the Inuit of the north is appreciated the world over as bold and unique.

Here is a Haida drawing of a killer whale. the interior designs are floating around the whale. Write the numbers in the boxes to match the parts in the drawing.

NEWFOUNDLAND AND LABRADOR

BEC

The city of Montreal is the second largest French-speaking city in the world (the largest is Paris, France). Although it is a modern city of almost 3,000,000 people, much of the older center of the city has been preserved, giving Montreal a very European look and feel.

PRINCE EDWARD ISLAND

Halifax

NOVA SCOTIA

Montreal

NEW BRUNSWICK

The CN Tower in Toronto, Ontario is the tallest free-standing structure in the Western Hemisphere attracting more than 2,000,000 visitors every year.

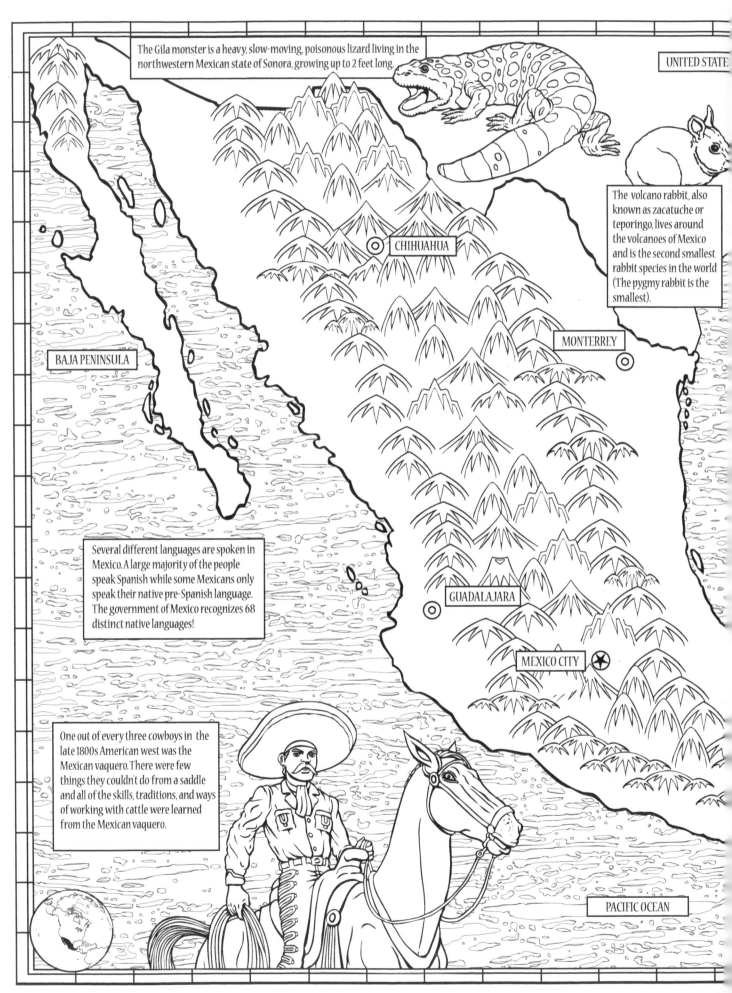

The Gila monster is a heavy, slow-moving, poisonous lizard living in the northwestern Mexican state of Sonora, growing up to 2 feet long.

UNITED STATE

The volcano rabbit, also known as zacatuche or teporingo, lives around the volcanoes of Mexico and is the second smallest rabbit species in the world (The pygmy rabbit is the smallest).

CHIHUAHUA

MONTERREY

BAJA PENINSULA

Several different languages are spoken in Mexico. A large majority of the people speak Spanish while some Mexicans only speak their native pre-Spanish language. The government of Mexico recognizes 68 distinct native languages!

GUADALAJARA

MEXICO CITY

One out of every three cowboys in the late 1800s American west was the Mexican vaquero. There were few things they couldn't do from a saddle and all of the skills, traditions, and ways of working with cattle were learned from the Mexican vaquero.

PACIFIC OCEAN

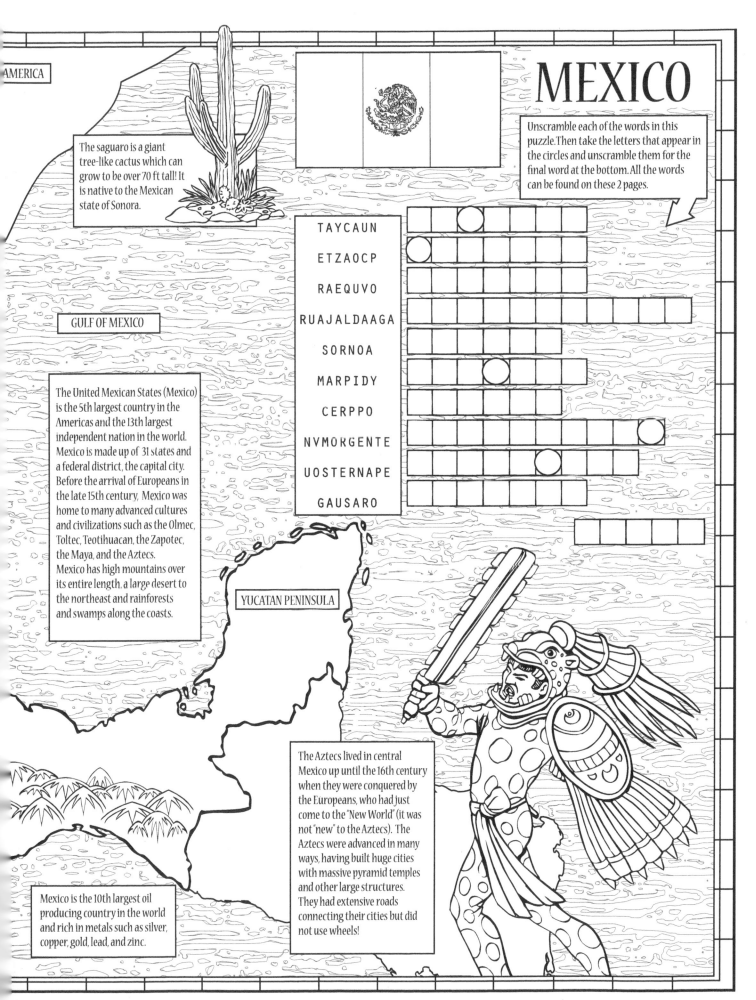

AMERICA

The saguaro is a giant tree-like cactus which can grow to be over 70 ft tall! It is native to the Mexican state of Sonora.

Unscramble each of the words in this puzzle. Then take the letters that appear in the circles and unscramble them for the final word at the bottom. All the words can be found on these 2 pages.

GULF OF MEXICO

TAYCAUN

ETZAOCP

RAEQUVO

RUAJALDAAGA

SORNOA

MARPIDY

CERPPO

NVMORGENTE

UOSTERNAPE

GAUSARO

The United Mexican States (Mexico) is the 5th largest country in the Americas and the 13th largest independent nation in the world. Mexico is made up of 31 states and a federal district, the capital city. Before the arrival of Europeans in the late 15th century, Mexico was home to many advanced cultures and civilizations such as the Olmec, Toltec, Teotihuacan, the Zapotec, the Maya, and the Aztecs. Mexico has high mountains over its entire length, a large desert to the northeast and rainforests and swamps along the coasts.

YUCATAN PENINSULA

The Aztecs lived in central Mexico up until the 16th century when they were conquered by the Europeans, who had just come to the "New World" (it was not "new" to the Aztecs). The Aztecs were advanced in many ways, having built huge cities with massive pyramid temples and other large structures. They had extensive roads connecting their cities but did not use wheels!

Mexico is the 10th largest oil producing country in the world and rich in metals such as silver, copper, gold, lead, and zinc.

The Maya were amazing artists and left us many wonderful sculptures, carvings, and wall paintings. There are 12 sculptures below. Can you find 2 that are identical?

MEXICO

Caracara Bird

Central America has majestic mountains, awesome rainforests, mysterious jungle swamps and large open fields and marshes. But its most interesting feature is not natural; the countries of Honduras, Guatemala, El Salvador, and Belize are dotted with hundreds of buildings, small and large (some very large), mostly shaped like pyramids.

They were built by a people known as the Maya. This nation existed between 2,000 BC and 900 AD. They built large cities (some may have had as many as 150,000 people!) all over this region, and had an advanced knowledge of sciences and mathematics.

The Maya are one of the great mysteries of history: 500 years before the arrival of Columbus and other explorers, the Maya abandoned their massive cities and went back to the jungle. No one really knows why.

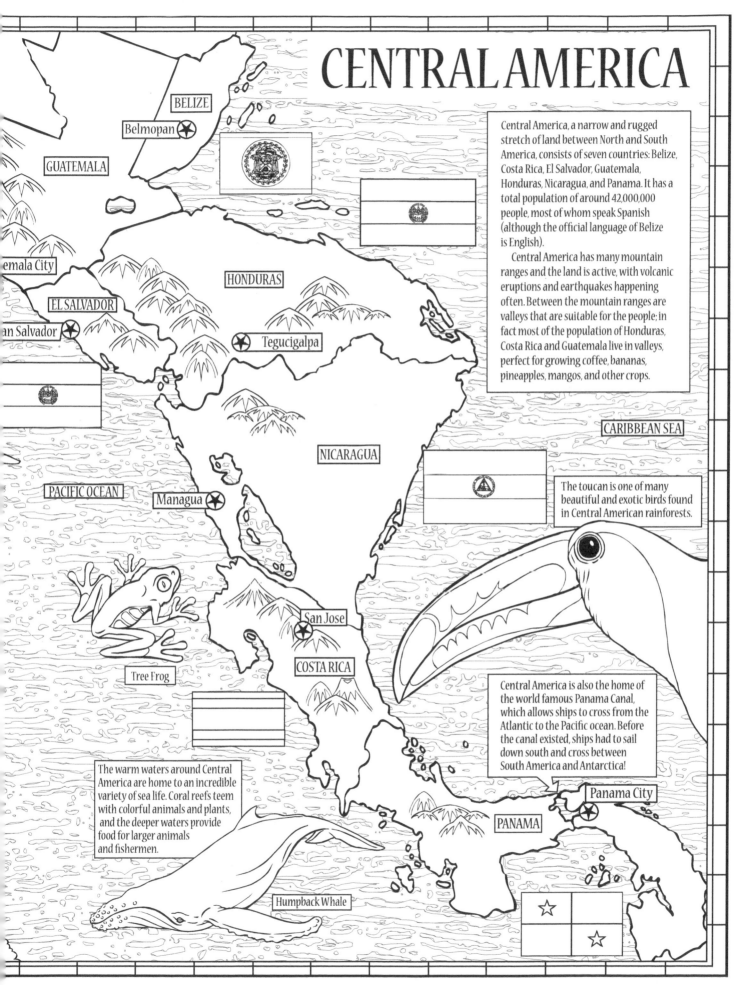

CENTRAL AMERICA

BELIZE

Belmopan ✦

GUATEMALA

emala City

HONDURAS

EL SALVADOR

an Salvador ✦

Tegucigalpa ✦

NICARAGUA

PACIFIC OCEAN

Managua ✦

CARIBBEAN SEA

Tree Frog

San Jose ✦

COSTA RICA

Humpback Whale

PANAMA

Panama City ✦

Central America, a narrow and rugged stretch of land between North and South America, consists of seven countries: Belize, Costa Rica, El Salvador, Guatemala, Honduras, Nicaragua, and Panama. It has a total population of around 42,000,000 people, most of whom speak Spanish (although the official language of Belize is English).

Central America has many mountain ranges and the land is active, with volcanic eruptions and earthquakes happening often. Between the mountain ranges are valleys that are suitable for the people; in fact most of the population of Honduras, Costa Rica and Guatemala live in valleys, perfect for growing coffee, bananas, pineapples, mangos, and other crops.

The toucan is one of many beautiful and exotic birds found in Central American rainforests.

Central America is also the home of the world famous Panama Canal, which allows ships to cross from the Atlantic to the Pacific ocean. Before the canal existed, ships had to sail down south and cross between South America and Antarctica!

The warm waters around Central America are home to an incredible variety of sea life. Coral reefs teem with colorful animals and plants, and the deeper waters provide food for larger animals and fishermen.

Before North and South America were discovered by people from across the Atlantic Ocean, the Caribbean islands were inhabited by three different peoples: the Arawaks, the Caribs, and the Ciboney. These tribes slowly disappeared as more Europeans came to take over their lands. Christopher Columbus was the first European to visit several of the islands (in 1492). In 1496 the first permanent European settlement was made by Spain on Hispaniola (Haiti and Dominican Republic). By the middle 1600s England, France, and Holland had towns and trade posts in the area, and in the following century there was constant war between these countries for control of the islands. Some islands became important trade centers and were attacked by pirates! Large numbers of Africans were brought in as slaves to work the sugarcane plantations and other hard labor.

LANGUAGES OF THE CARIBBEAN ISLANDS:
English
French
Dutch
Spanish
French Creole
Patois Creole

BAHAMAS

CUBA

CAYMAN ISLANDS

JAMAICA

HAITI

Playful bottlenose dolphins are found all over the Caribbean.

Can you find these island names in the word puzzle?
BAHAMAS, CUBA, JAMAICA, HAITI
DOMINICAN REPUBLIC, PUERTO RICO
GUADELOUPE, MARTINIQUE,
SAINT VINCENT, BARBADOS, GRENADA,
TRINIDAD, TOBAGO, CAYMAN, ARUBA,
VIRGIN ISLANDS, BERMUDA

BERMUDA

CARIBBEA
SEA

```
P G N S I F D C Q R O C U B A E J F Q V
Q K W C R A O T X C C G R F T X P G Z D
A N K P U E R T O R I C O Y O L U L T S
B W T T W I X Y Z U I Q T A G A C Z J U
U C T K N X Z M T C N N D M D R Z I H V
R H Q I Z C R F T V S U T E C V S Q X C
A G D P W A W B D M M N L B I T M A Q B
V A Z M I Y S E B R E O E R E A X C S M
D O A Q V M H J E C U B G E V I F Y B R
B A R X Z A W B N P A I D U D S A N Z U
A O C K B N D I E C N S T Q H B E Y S F
H U C I M B V R A I O Q J I N R O X O Y
A M A Q A T Z X S H P U V N L J N Y F Y
M O I D N M O L W J O B A I P G L K M Z
A L Y I A K A B C N E F I T I A H W B J
S J A O X N F J A G Q U G R C C W Z M O
K S D I D T E Z V S S O D A B R A B C L
T L Z S Y K I R A M O B N M U G U N S G
L I J W W R I B G W H M M H O S K F F I
Y K Z Y C Y I N L B J N V E H K Y B G
G C I L B U P E R N A C I N I M O D M Z
```

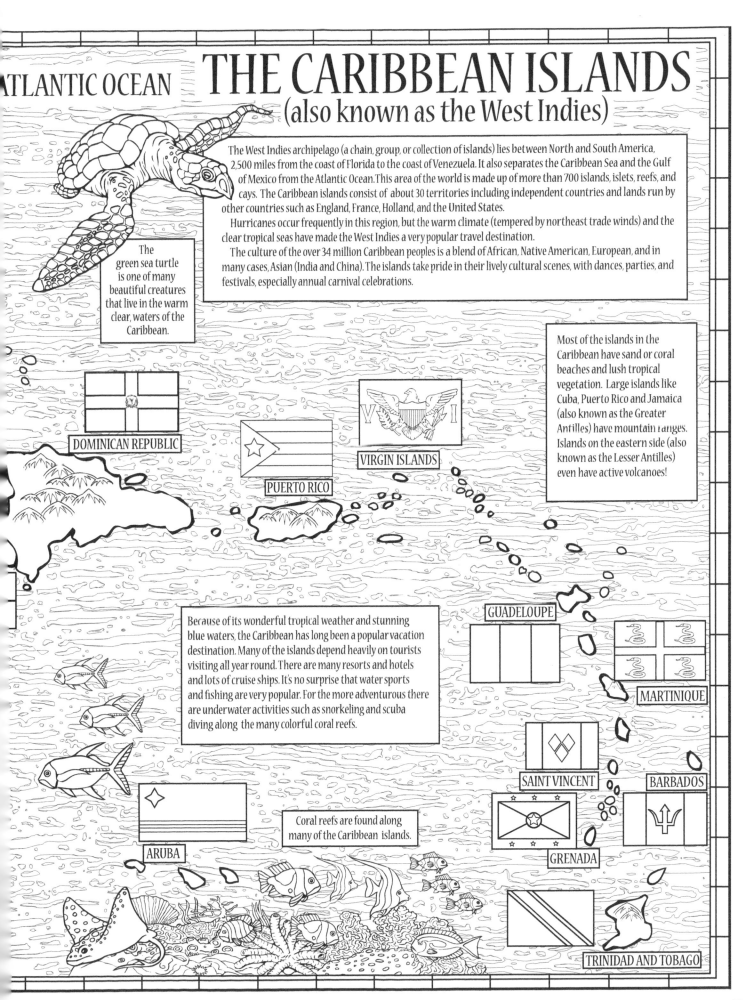

THE CARIBBEAN ISLANDS
(also known as the West Indies)

The West Indies archipelago (a chain, group, or collection of islands) lies between North and South America, 2,500 miles from the coast of Florida to the coast of Venezuela. It also separates the Caribbean Sea and the Gulf of Mexico from the Atlantic Ocean. This area of the world is made up of more than 700 islands, islets, reefs, and cays. The Caribbean islands consist of about 30 territories including independent countries and lands run by other countries such as England, France, Holland, and the United States.

Hurricanes occur frequently in this region, but the warm climate (tempered by northeast trade winds) and the clear tropical seas have made the West Indies a very popular travel destination.

The culture of the over 34 million Caribbean peoples is a blend of African, Native American, European, and in many cases, Asian (India and China). The islands take pride in their lively cultural scenes, with dances, parties, and festivals, especially annual carnival celebrations.

The green sea turtle is one of many beautiful creatures that live in the warm clear, waters of the Caribbean.

Most of the islands in the Caribbean have sand or coral beaches and lush tropical vegetation. Large islands like Cuba, Puerto Rico and Jamaica (also known as the Greater Antilles) have mountain ranges. Islands on the eastern side (also known as the Lesser Antilles) even have active volcanoes!

DOMINICAN REPUBLIC

PUERTO RICO

VIRGIN ISLANDS

GUADELOUPE

MARTINIQUE

Because of its wonderful tropical weather and stunning blue waters, the Caribbean has long been a popular vacation destination. Many of the islands depend heavily on tourists visiting all year round. There are many resorts and hotels and lots of cruise ships. It's no surprise that water sports and fishing are very popular. For the more adventurous there are underwater activities such as snorkeling and scuba diving along the many colorful coral reefs.

SAINT VINCENT

BARBADOS

ARUBA

Coral reefs are found along many of the Caribbean islands.

GRENADA

TRINIDAD AND TOBAGO

23

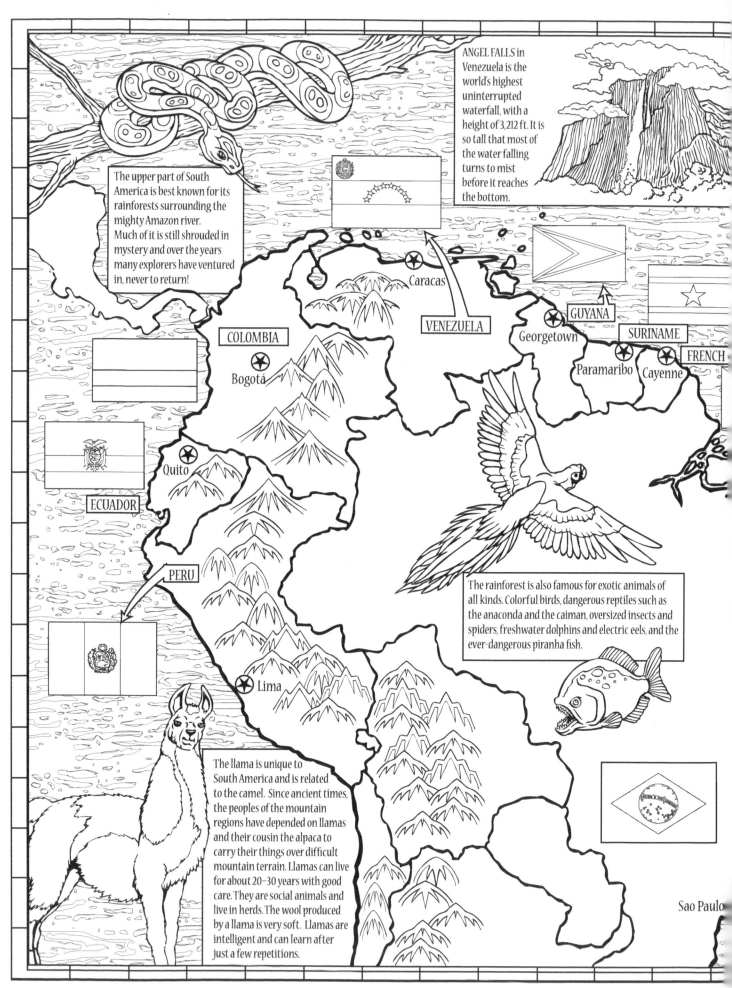

ANGEL FALLS in Venezuela is the world's highest uninterrupted waterfall, with a height of 3,212 ft. It is so tall that most of the water falling turns to mist before it reaches the bottom.

The upper part of South America is best known for its rainforests surrounding the mighty Amazon river. Much of it is still shrouded in mystery and over the years many explorers have ventured in, never to return!

VENEZUELA

Caracas

GUYANA

Georgetown

SURINAME

Paramaribo   Cayenne

FRENCH

COLOMBIA

Bogotá

Quito

ECUADOR

PERU

Lima

The rainforest is also famous for exotic animals of all kinds. Colorful birds, dangerous reptiles such as the anaconda and the caiman, oversized insects and spiders, freshwater dolphins and electric eels, and the ever-dangerous piranha fish.

The llama is unique to South America and is related to the camel. Since ancient times, the peoples of the mountain regions have depended on llamas and their cousin the alpaca to carry their things over difficult mountain terrain. Llamas can live for about 20–30 years with good care. They are social animals and live in herds. The wool produced by a llama is very soft. Llamas are intelligent and can learn after just a few repetitions.

Sao Paulo

SOUTH AMERICA (Top)

SOUTH AMERICA is bordered on the west by the Pacific Ocean and on the north and east by the Atlantic Ocean. Most of the people live near the western or eastern coasts of the continent while the middle and the far south have very few. There are many types of people in South America: cultures and peoples originating in South America as well as Europe, Africa, and Asia. As a result, most South Americans speak Spanish, with the exception of Brazil where most people speak Portuguese.

South Americans are passionate about their favorite sport, soccer (football). Some of the world's most famous players came from Brazil and Argentina, and both countries have dominated the sport for many years.

```
I S K A E M A N W Q M O R R Y W S I C J
P T E C W G U P M M E I Q M T H K A U I
L B O L E D S A O P A U L O O I P Q H C
V O K X P N B W E S A X P L P W D Q D C
E G B R K S N P W X U D K Z J E U K B
X O P G B J B U Z D P N B R A Y I Q E
B T Y H S F O Z P E H M B I W O T O N
U A V M V V J C Z E D W A O M B O X K
K O B C L E C A E C C I R D R I F O
H O Y B X A G Y N J X K D E R R V J
Y X I L M F N E B V K P I J A A T C
D C D I S I C N O K K A P A H M D L
K K L S F N E N T N F O O N M A I N
P E J K C X W E W N L E B E D R X W
A T R J Z M Y U E L S W C I E A L Y
C F G E O R G E T O W N C R L P L B
B B R A S I L I A T L D C O C Y Y
O A Y T Z J V V S E M U O V C J L
D U B L L D V K R R J H Q J W G A F
D J G V I Z T G K V J S O C A R A C
```

This puzzle contains the names of every city on this map. Can you find them?

BRAZIL

The Amazon rainforest represents over half of our planet's remaining rainforests. It is estimated that there are 16,000 varieties of trees totaling 390,000,000,000 individual trees!

The mysterious Nazca Lines are found in Peru. No one knows why these massive lines and drawings of animals were made.

South America contains more than 40 percent of the world's plants and animals species, but covers only 15 percent of the earth's land surface.

Brasilia

Largest city in the western hemisphere with over 11,000,000 people.

Rio de Janeiro

The Carnaval in Rio de Janeiro is a world famous festival held before Lent every year and considered the biggest carnival in the world with two million people per day on the streets.

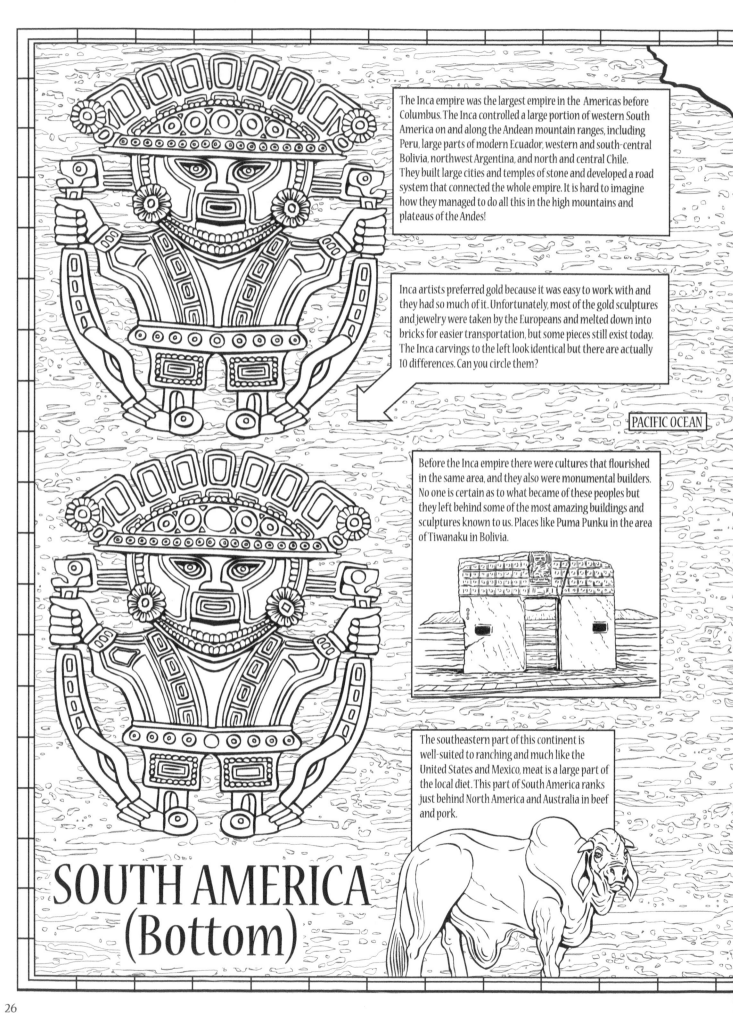

The Inca empire was the largest empire in the Americas before Columbus. The Inca controlled a large portion of western South America on and along the Andean mountain ranges, including Peru, large parts of modern Ecuador, western and south-central Bolivia, northwest Argentina, and north and central Chile. They built large cities and temples of stone and developed a road system that connected the whole empire. It is hard to imagine how they managed to do all this in the high mountains and plateaus of the Andes!

Inca artists preferred gold because it was easy to work with and they had so much of it. Unfortunately, most of the gold sculptures and jewelry were taken by the Europeans and melted down into bricks for easier transportation, but some pieces still exist today. The Inca carvings to the left look identical but there are actually 10 differences. Can you circle them?

PACIFIC OCEAN

Before the Inca empire there were cultures that flourished in the same area, and they also were monumental builders. No one is certain as to what became of these peoples but they left behind some of the most amazing buildings and sculptures known to us. Places like Puma Punku in the area of Tiwanaku in Bolivia.

The southeastern part of this continent is well-suited to ranching and much like the United States and Mexico, meat is a large part of the local diet. This part of South America ranks just behind North America and Australia in beef and pork.

SOUTH AMERICA (Bottom)

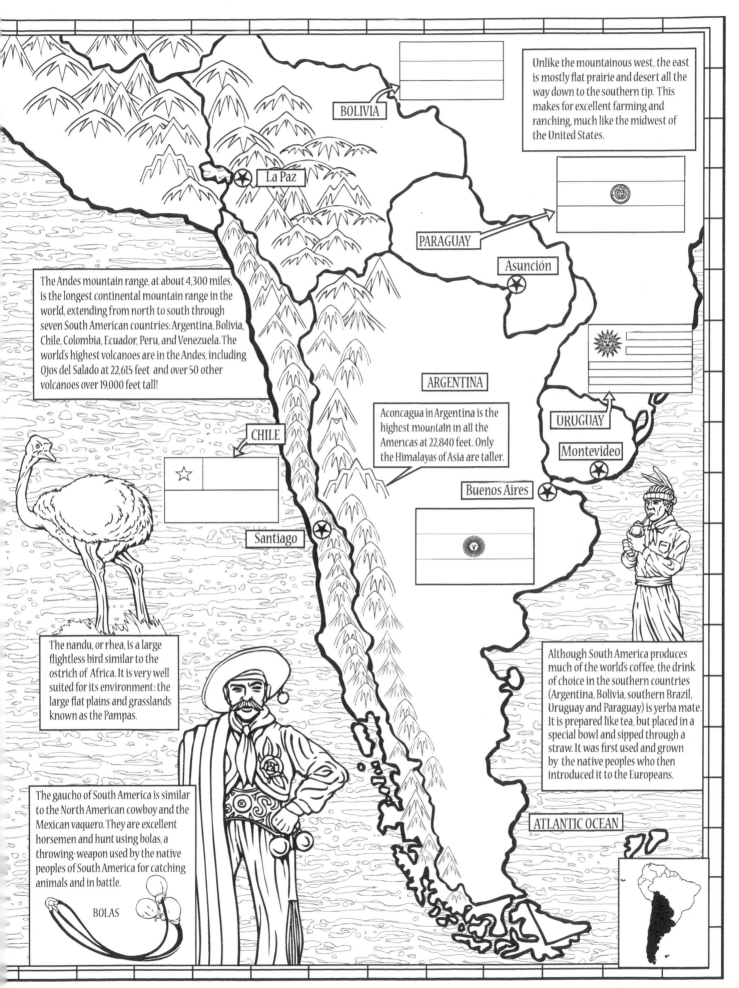

BOLIVIA

Unlike the mountainous west, the east is mostly flat prairie and desert all the way down to the southern tip. This makes for excellent farming and ranching, much like the midwest of the United States.

La Paz

PARAGUAY

Asunción

The Andes mountain range, at about 4,300 miles, is the longest continental mountain range in the world, extending from north to south through seven South American countries: Argentina, Bolivia, Chile, Colombia, Ecuador, Peru, and Venezuela. The world's highest volcanoes are in the Andes, including Ojos del Salado at 22,615 feet and over 50 other volcanoes over 19,000 feet tall!

ARGENTINA

Aconcagua in Argentina is the highest mountain in all the Americas at 22,840 feet. Only the Himalayas of Asia are taller.

URUGUAY

CHILE

Montevideo

Buenos Aires

Santiago

The nandu, or rhea, is a large flightless bird similar to the ostrich of Africa. It is very well suited for its environment: the large flat plains and grasslands known as the Pampas.

Although South America produces much of the world's coffee, the drink of choice in the southern countries (Argentina, Bolivia, southern Brazil, Uruguay and Paraguay) is yerba mate. It is prepared like tea, but placed in a special bowl and sipped through a straw. It was first used and grown by the native peoples who then introduced it to the Europeans.

The gaucho of South America is similar to the North American cowboy and the Mexican vaquero. They are excellent horsemen and hunt using bolas, a throwing-weapon used by the native peoples of South America for catching animals and in battle.

BOLAS

ATLANTIC OCEAN

27

EASTERN HEMISPHERE

The Eastern Hemisphere is the half of the earth that contains Europe, Asia, Africa, Indonesia, Australia and most of the Pacific Islands. This hemisphere is also called the Old World, as many of the civilizations in the east go back thousands of years.

The landmass of the Eastern Hemisphere is greater than the Western Hemisphere and has more than 5 times the population.

ATLANT

The dragon is a symbol used by many cultures in east Asia.

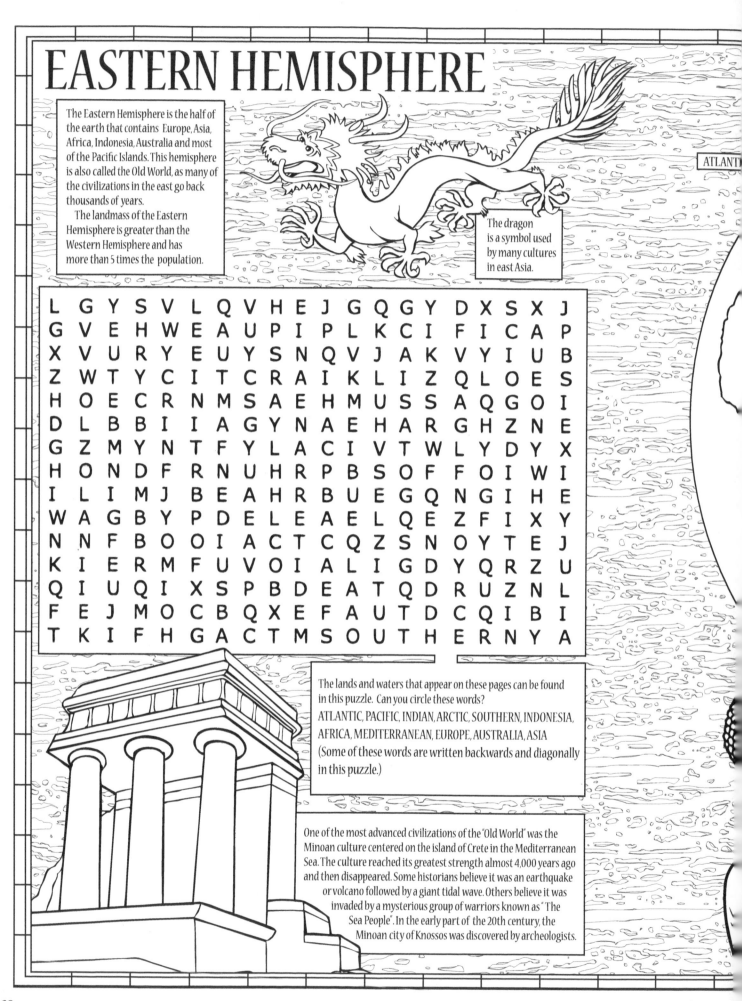

```
L G Y S V L Q V H E J G Q G Y D X S X J
G V E H W E A U P I P L K C I F I C A P
X V U R Y E U Y S N Q V J A K V Y I U B
Z W T Y C I T C R A I K L I Z Q L O E S
H O E C R N M S A E H M U S S A Q G O I
D L B B I I A G Y N A E H A R G H Z N E
G Z M Y N T F Y L A C I V T W L Y D Y X
H O N D F R N U H R P B S O F F O I W I
I L I M J B E A H R B U E G Q N G I H E
W A G B Y P D E L E A E L Q E Z F I X Y
N N F B O O I A C T C Q Z S N O Y T E J
K I E R M F U V O I A L I G D Y Q R Z U
Q I U Q I X S P B D E A T Q D R U Z N L
F E J M O C B Q X E F A U T D C Q I B I
T K I F H G A C T M S O U T H E R N Y A
```

The lands and waters that appear on these pages can be found in this puzzle. Can you circle these words?
ATLANTIC, PACIFIC, INDIAN, ARCTIC, SOUTHERN, INDONESIA, AFRICA, MEDITERRANEAN, EUROPE, AUSTRALIA, ASIA
(Some of these words are written backwards and diagonally in this puzzle.)

One of the most advanced civilizations of the "Old World" was the Minoan culture centered on the island of Crete in the Mediterranean Sea. The culture reached its greatest strength almost 4,000 years ago and then disappeared. Some historians believe it was an earthquake or volcano followed by a giant tidal wave. Others believe it was invaded by a mysterious group of warriors known as "The Sea People". In the early part of the 20th century, the Minoan city of Knossos was discovered by archeologists.

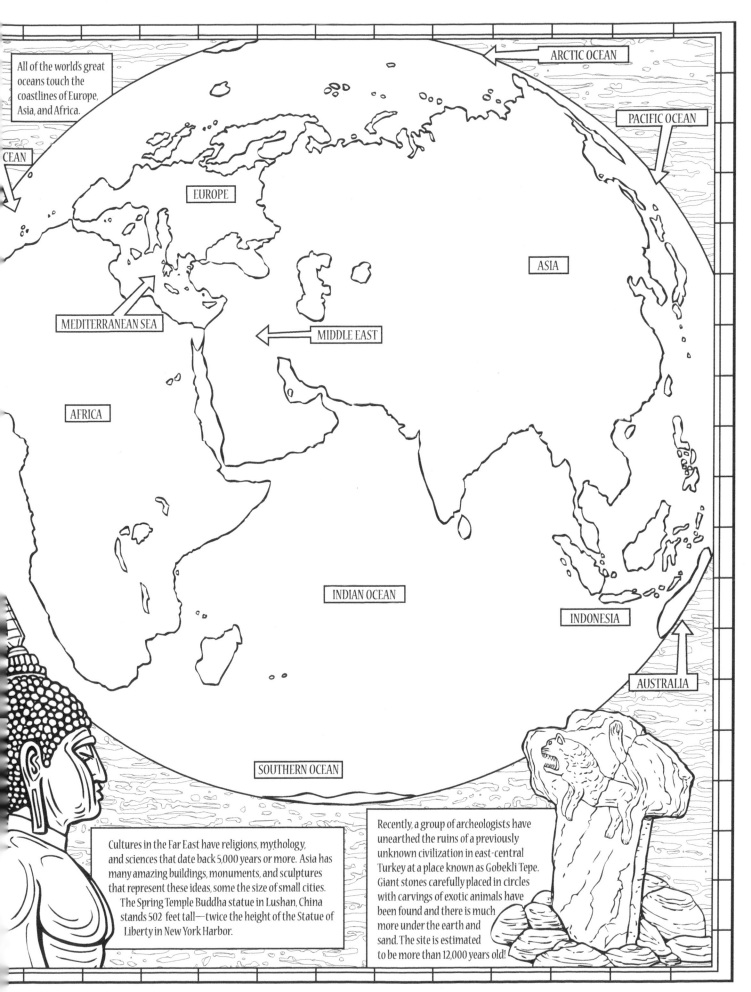

All of the world's great oceans touch the coastlines of Europe, Asia, and Africa.

ARCTIC OCEAN

PACIFIC OCEAN

CEAN

EUROPE

ASIA

MEDITERRANEAN SEA

MIDDLE EAST

AFRICA

INDIAN OCEAN

INDONESIA

AUSTRALIA

SOUTHERN OCEAN

Cultures in the Far East have religions, mythology, and sciences that date back 5,000 years or more. Asia has many amazing buildings, monuments, and sculptures that represent these ideas, some the size of small cities. The Spring Temple Buddha statue in Lushan, China stands 502 feet tall—twice the height of the Statue of Liberty in New York Harbor.

Recently, a group of archeologists have unearthed the ruins of a previously unknown civilization in east-central Turkey at a place known as Gobekli Tepe. Giant stones carefully placed in circles with carvings of exotic animals have been found and there is much more under the earth and sand. The site is estimated to be more than 12,000 years old!

EUROPE

Although connected to Asia as one large continental landmass, Europe is considered a continent on its own. From the end of the 15th century to the beginning of the 20th, European culture dominated the entire world and many areas still reflect this fact. North and South America are very much an extended European culture with major influences of English, French, Spanish, Portugese, and German. There are 50 countries in Europe and almost as many official languages.

Most countries in Europe belong to an organization called the European Union which allows easier travel and trade, and use of the same kind of money, the Euro.

Travel between Europe and the "New World" began long before Columbus. Monks and Vikings had crossed over to Iceland and Greenland over 1,000 years ago. Here's a depiction from Ireland of men rowing a large boat on the ocean. This image has been cut into 21 pieces and then scrambled. Can you match the numbers to the scattered pieces?

The Gulf Stream, an ocean current that crosses the Atlantic from around the Caribbean Sea up to the European continent, brings warmer water and climate, making European winters slightly milder.

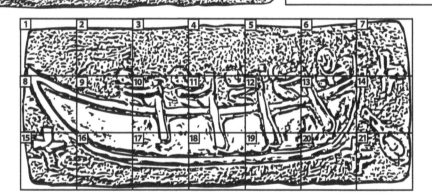

ATLANTIC OCEAN

From the 19th century to the late 20th century, over 60,000,000 Europeans left their homes and crossed the ocean to the Americas.

30

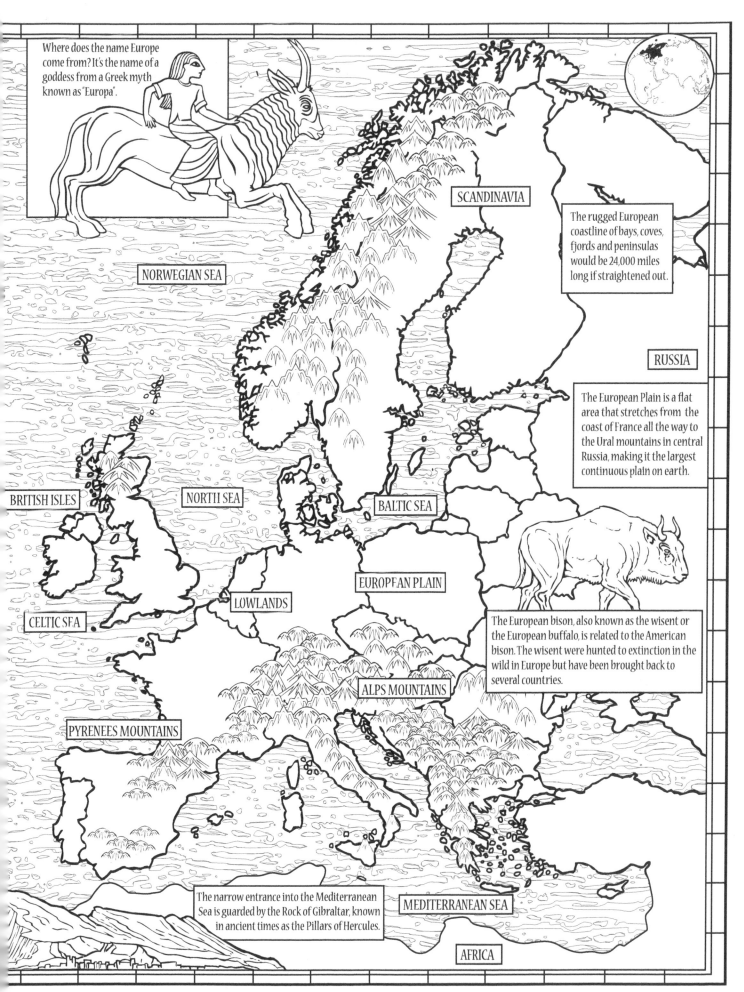

Where does the name Europe come from? It's the name of a goddess from a Greek myth known as "Europa".

NORWEGIAN SEA

SCANDINAVIA

The rugged European coastline of bays, coves, fjords and peninsulas would be 24,000 miles long if straightened out.

RUSSIA

The European Plain is a flat area that stretches from the coast of France all the way to the Ural mountains in central Russia, making it the largest continuous plain on earth.

BRITISH ISLES

NORTH SEA

BALTIC SEA

CELTIC SEA

LOWLANDS

EUROPEAN PLAIN

The European bison, also known as the wisent or the European buffalo, is related to the American bison. The wisent were hunted to extinction in the wild in Europe but have been brought back to several countries.

PYRENEES MOUNTAINS

ALPS MOUNTAINS

The narrow entrance into the Mediterranean Sea is guarded by the Rock of Gibraltar, known in ancient times as the Pillars of Hercules.

MEDITERRANEAN SEA

AFRICA

NORTHERN EUROPE (and Major Cities)

During an era known as the "Dark Ages" that began after the fall of Rome in the 5th century AD, much of the knowledge of earlier times was preserved by monks living far away from society. They hand-lettered and protected copies of important books on history, philosophy, science, and medicine for future generations.

Northern Europe has a broad variety of natural and man-made features. There is the Great Plain of Europe, good for farming and raising cattle, the northern edge of the Alps mountain range, fertile river valleys of the Rhine, Rhone, Seine and Danube rivers, even land that is below sea level and has to be protected by sea walls (dykes), and Scandinavia with its rugged mountains and fjords.

And because of the general success of trade and industry over several hundred years, there are beautiful grand buildings and monuments in the great cities of the region.

ICELAND

Reykjavik

FAROE

FUHSRKTORSESRSEA

RRTSOSPETCEECATHL

HAISESCTENLCWR

HACSOSBALLAGREUT

CELTEBNOLNALRUSTAC

MANGITROSELOBAL

DESNATOLMETLEC

Unscramble each of the clue words (each clue word is a castle name found on this page). Copy the letters in the numbered boxes to the same numbered box in the row above, and you will discover the bonus word (also found on this page).

Castles can be seen all over northern Europe, massive symbols of a past age. The castle began as raised walls of earth and rocks, but over time became the ultimate military achievement. In Scandinavia, Central Europe, and the British Isles stood walled fortresses surrounding a castle keep (which was the last line of defense) with names like AKERSHUS FORTRESS, PORTCHESTER CASTLE, SCHWERIN CASTLE, AALBORGHUS CASTLE, ACTON BURNELL CASTLE, AMALIENBORG SLOT, CASTEL DEL MONTE.

The castles fell out of use once they could no longer defend against bigger and more powerful cannons and rifles that could shoot further.

IRELA
Du

ATLANTIC OCEAN

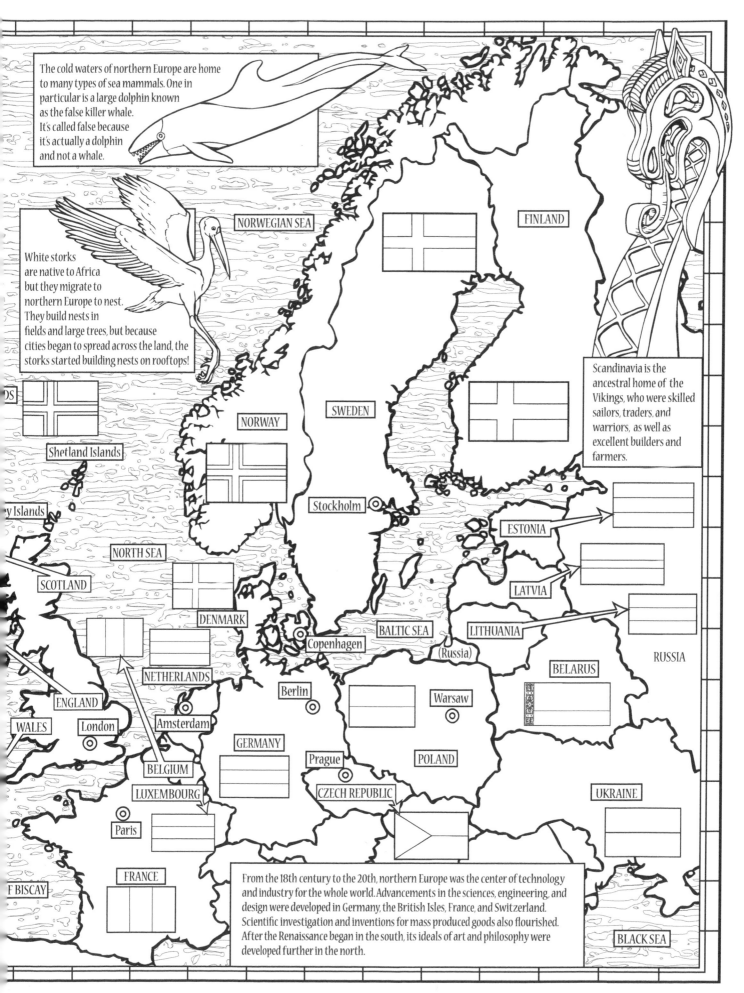

The cold waters of northern Europe are home to many types of sea mammals. One in particular is a large dolphin known as the false killer whale. It's called false because it's actually a dolphin and not a whale.

White storks are native to Africa but they migrate to northern Europe to nest. They build nests in fields and large trees, but because cities began to spread across the land, the storks started building nests on rooftops!

Scandinavia is the ancestral home of the Vikings, who were skilled sailors, traders, and warriors, as well as excellent builders and farmers.

From the 18th century to the 20th, northern Europe was the center of technology and industry for the whole world. Advancements in the sciences, engineering, and design were developed in Germany, the British Isles, France, and Switzerland. Scientific investigation and inventions for mass produced goods also flourished. After the Renaissance began in the south, its ideals of art and philosophy were developed further in the north.

NORWEGIAN SEA

FINLAND

SWEDEN

NORWAY

Shetland Islands

y Islands

NORTH SEA

SCOTLAND

Stockholm

ESTONIA

LATVIA

LITHUANIA

(Russia)

RUSSIA

BELARUS

DENMARK

BALTIC SEA

Copenhagen

NETHERLANDS

Berlin

Warsaw

ENGLAND

London

Amsterdam

WALES

BELGIUM

GERMANY

Prague

POLAND

LUXEMBOURG

CZECH REPUBLIC

UKRAINE

Paris

FRANCE

F BISCAY

BLACK SEA

DS

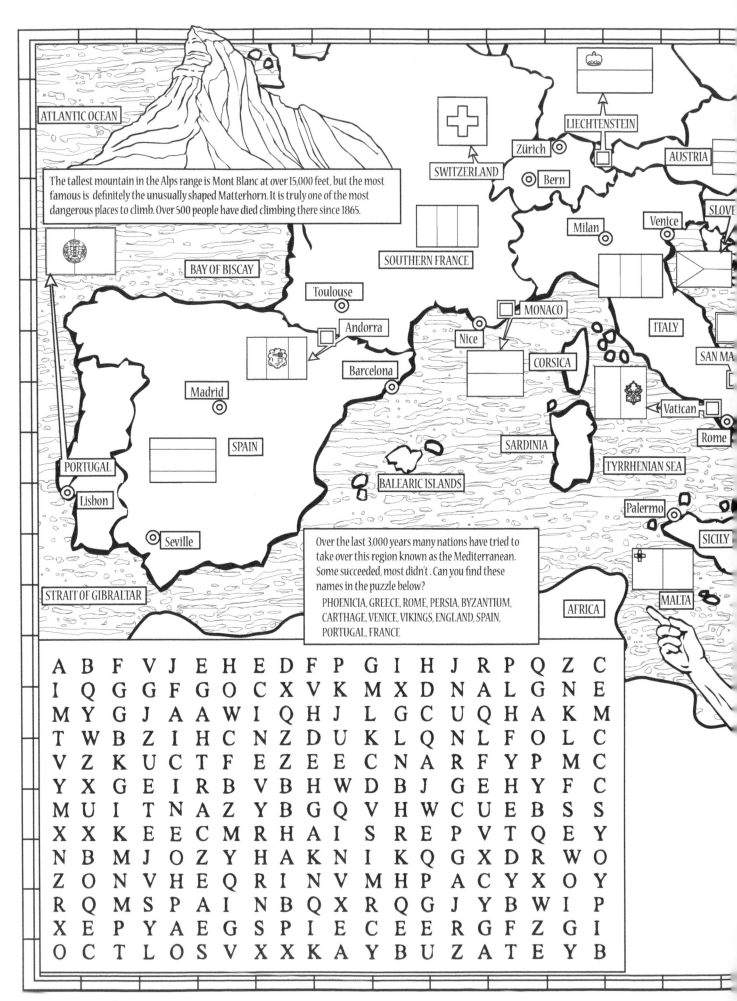

ATLANTIC OCEAN

The tallest mountain in the Alps range is Mont Blanc at over 15,000 feet, but the most famous is definitely the unusually shaped Matterhorn. It is truly one of the most dangerous places to climb. Over 500 people have died climbing there since 1865.

BAY OF BISCAY

SWITZERLAND

Zürich

Bern

LIECHTENSTEIN

AUSTRIA

SOUTHERN FRANCE

SLOVE

Venice

Milan

Toulouse

Andorra

MONACO

Nice

CORSICA

ITALY

SAN MA

Barcelona

Madrid

Vatican

SPAIN

Rome

SARDINIA

PORTUGAL

TYRRHENIAN SEA

Lisbon

BALEARIC ISLANDS

Palermo

Seville

SICILY

STRAIT OF GIBRALTAR

Over the last 3,000 years many nations have tried to take over this region known as the Mediterranean. Some succeeded, most didn't. Can you find these names in the puzzle below?

PHOENICIA, GREECE, ROME, PERSIA, BYZANTIUM, CARTHAGE, VENICE, VIKINGS, ENGLAND, SPAIN, PORTUGAL, FRANCE

AFRICA

MALTA

```
A B F V J E H E D F P G I H J R P Q Z C
I Q G G F G O C X V K M X D N A L G N E
M Y G J A A W I Q H J L G C U Q H A K M
T W B Z I H C N Z D U K L Q N L F O L C
V Z K U C T F E Z E E C N A R F Y P M C
Y X G E I R B V B H W D B J G E H Y F S
M U I T N A Z Y B G Q V H W C U E B S S
X X K E E C M R H A I S R E P V T Q E Y
N B M J O Z Y H A K N I K Q G X D R W O
Z O N V H E Q R I N V M H P A C Y X O Y
R Q M S P A I N B Q X R Q G J Y B W I P
X E P Y A E G S P I E C E E R G F Z G I
O C T L O S V X X K A Y B U Z A T E Y B
```

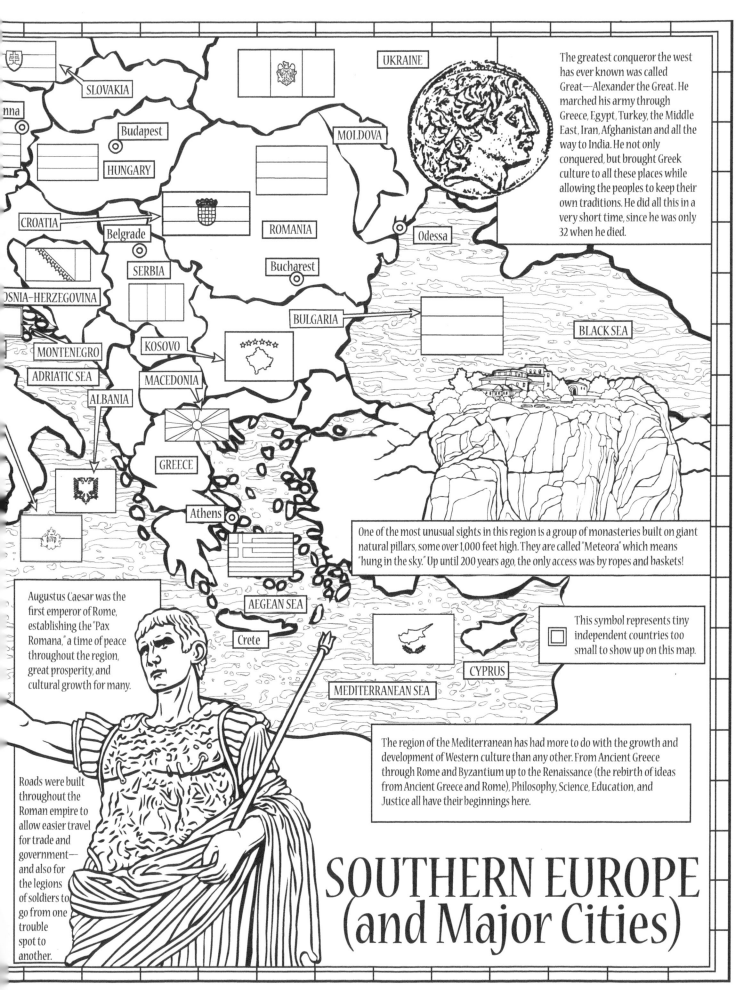

SLOVAKIA

Budapest

HUNGARY

CROATIA

Belgrade

SERBIA

BOSNIA-HERZEGOVINA

MONTENEGRO

ADRIATIC SEA

KOSOVO

MACEDONIA

ALBANIA

GREECE

Athens

AEGEAN SEA

Crete

UKRAINE

MOLDOVA

ROMANIA

Bucharest

Odessa

BULGARIA

BLACK SEA

CYPRUS

MEDITERRANEAN SEA

The greatest conqueror the west has ever known was called Great—Alexander the Great. He marched his army through Greece, Egypt, Turkey, the Middle East, Iran, Afghanistan and all the way to India. He not only conquered, but brought Greek culture to all these places while allowing the peoples to keep their own traditions. He did all this in a very short time, since he was only 32 when he died.

One of the most unusual sights in this region is a group of monasteries built on giant natural pillars, some over 1,000 feet high. They are called "Meteora" which means "hung in the sky." Up until 200 years ago, the only access was by ropes and baskets!

This symbol represents tiny independent countries too small to show up on this map.

Augustus Caesar was the first emperor of Rome, establishing the "Pax Romana," a time of peace throughout the region, great prosperity, and cultural growth for many.

The region of the Mediterranean has had more to do with the growth and development of Western culture than any other. From Ancient Greece through Rome and Byzantium up to the Renaissance (the rebirth of ideas from Ancient Greece and Rome), Philosophy, Science, Education, and Justice all have their beginnings here.

Roads were built throughout the Roman empire to allow easier travel for trade and government—and also for the legions of soldiers to go from one trouble spot to another.

SOUTHERN EUROPE
(and Major Cities)

The MIDDLE EAST (and Major Cities)

A very common sight in the middle east is the Minaret, a tower from which calls to prayer and announcements are made.

The Middle East can truly be called the "Cradle of Civilization". Archaeologists are daily uncovering evidence of cultures and societies with advanced building and engineering skills as old as 12,000 years! Even though much of the Middle East we know today is desert and rocky wilderness, historians suggest that much of the area was once green and able to sustain lots of people with fruit and grains grown in the region. Today most people live on the fringes of the wasteland, along the seacoast or the remaining rivers in the area.

Over the last 200 years archaeologists have dug up parts of cities long believed to be either completely lost or local legends that never existed. After Heinrich Schliemann discovered the lost city of Troy, work was begun to find other so-called lost cities: the Kingdom of the Hittites, the city of Nineveh, Ebla, Ur of the Chaldees, and many more continue to be unearthed.

Istanbul

TURKEY

CYPRUS

MEDITERRANEAN SEA

LEB

IS

Tel Avi

Alexandria

Jerusale

Cairo

Sina

EGYPT

Now imagine you have spent the day digging up a lost city and it's beginning to get dark. Can you find your way out before it's too late?

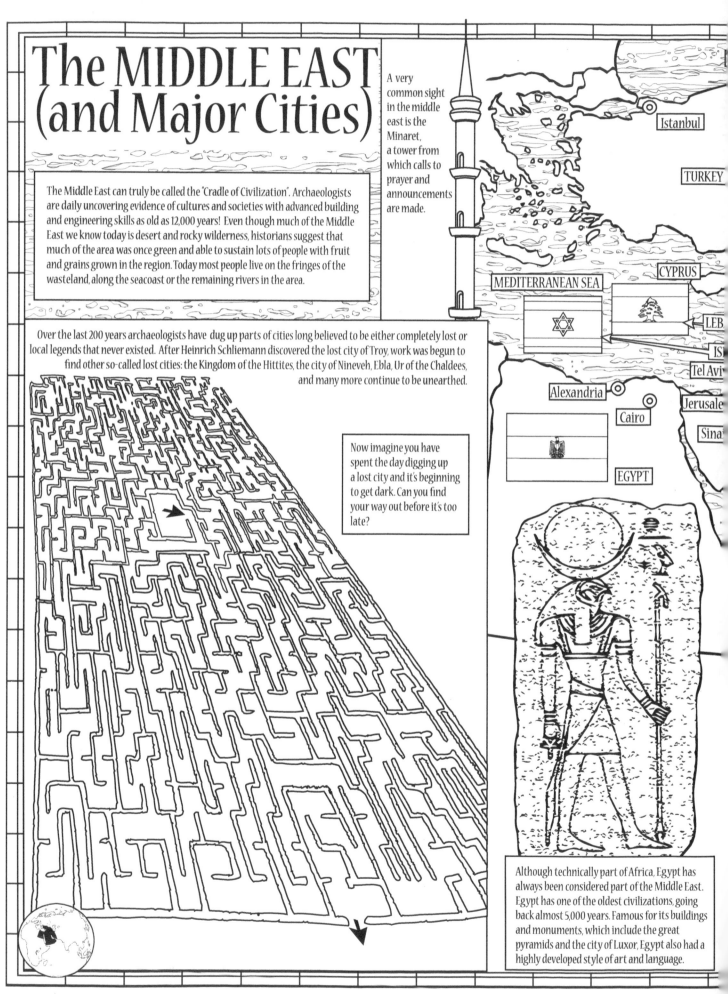

Although technically part of Africa, Egypt has always been considered part of the Middle East. Egypt has one of the oldest civilizations, going back almost 5,000 years. Famous for its buildings and monuments, which include the great pyramids and the city of Luxor, Egypt also had a highly developed style of art and language.

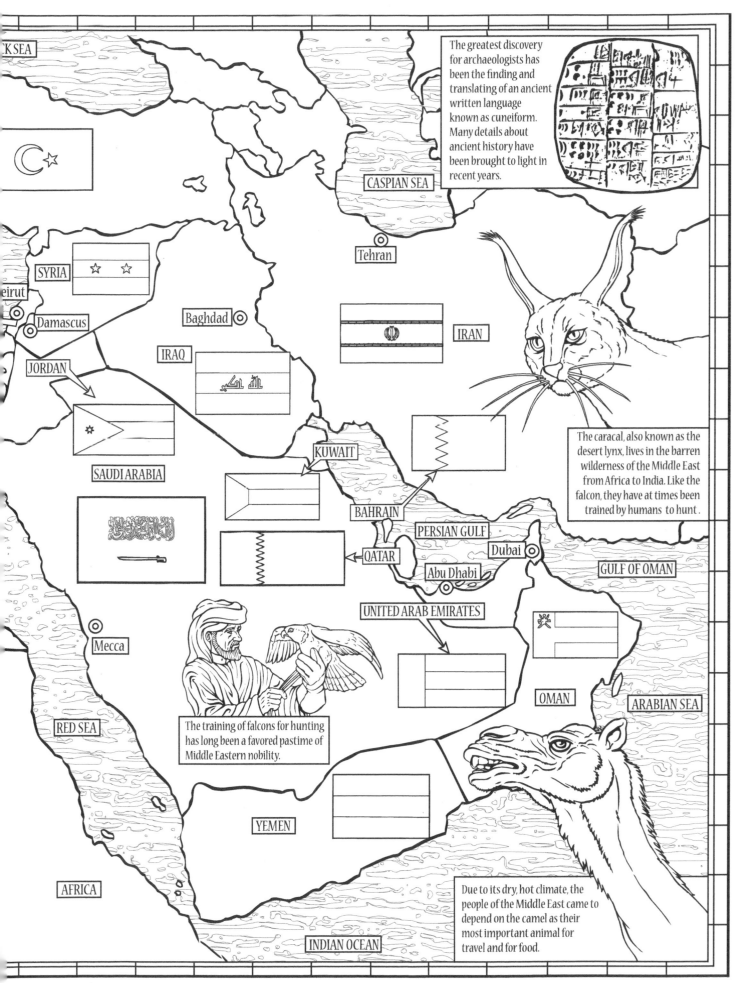

The greatest discovery for archaeologists has been the finding and translating of an ancient written language known as cuneiform. Many details about ancient history have been brought to light in recent years.

CASPIAN SEA

Tehran ⊚

SYRIA ☆ ☆

Beirut ⊚

Damascus ⊚

Baghdad ⊚

IRAN

JORDAN

IRAQ

SAUDI ARABIA

KUWAIT

BAHRAIN

PERSIAN GULF

QATAR

The caracal, also known as the desert lynx, lives in the barren wilderness of the Middle East from Africa to India. Like the falcon, they have at times been trained by humans to hunt.

Dubai ⊚

Abu Dhabi ⊚

GULF OF OMAN

UNITED ARAB EMIRATES

OMAN

ARABIAN SEA

Mecca ⊚

The training of falcons for hunting has long been a favored pastime of Middle Eastern nobility.

RED SEA

YEMEN

AFRICA

Due to its dry, hot climate, the people of the Middle East came to depend on the camel as their most important animal for travel and for food.

INDIAN OCEAN

37

ASIA

Asia is the largest continent on our planet and has the most people. In fact, almost 2 out of every 3 people in the world are Asian! Although Asia is connected to Europe as one continuous landmass (Eurasia), it's believed to begin east of the Black Sea. Asia is surrounded by the Pacific Ocean to the east, the Indian Ocean to the south, and the Arctic Ocean to the north. The largest forests in the world are in the north and the world's tallest mountains are in the south.

Asia has 2,269 languages, spoken by nearly 4 billion people. China and India each have over a billion people. China has 235 recognized languages and India has 114.

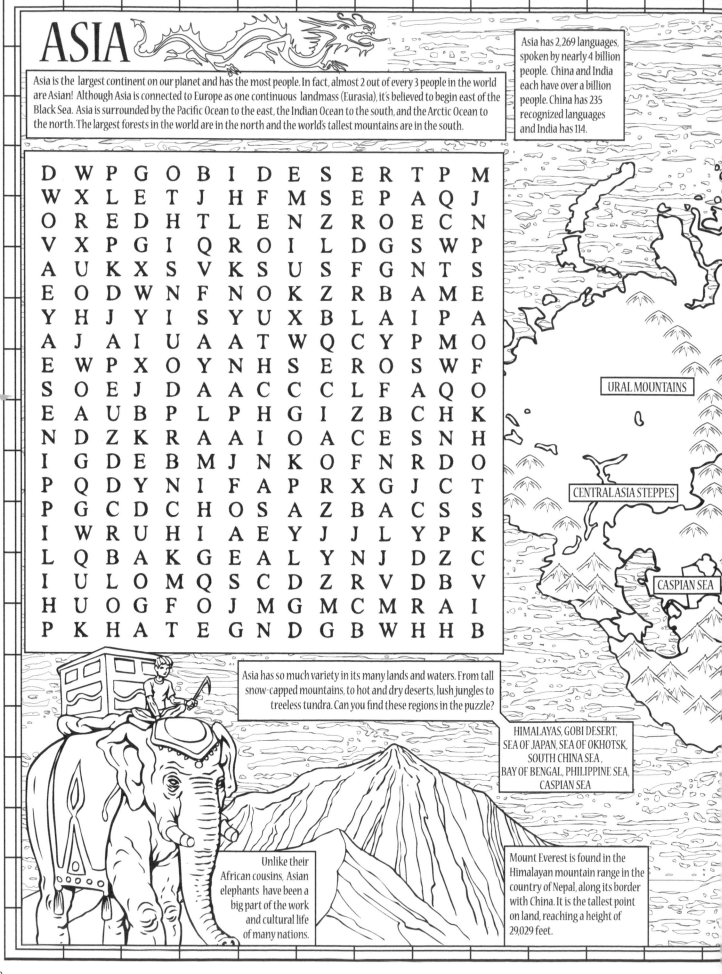

```
D W P G O B I D E S E R T P M
W X L E T J H F M S E P A Q J
O R E D H T L E N Z R O E C N
V X P G I Q R O I L D G S W P
A U K X S V K S U S F G N T S
E O D W N F N O K Z R B A M E
Y H J Y I S Y U X B L A I P A
A J A I U A A T W Q C Y P M O
E W P X O Y N H S E R O S W F
S O E J D A A C C L F A Q O
E A U B P L P H G I Z B C H K
N D Z K R A A I O A C E S N H
I G D E B M J N K O F N R D O
P Q D Y N I F A P R X G J C T
P G C D C H O S A Z B A C S S
I W R U H I A E Y J J L Y P K
L Q B A K G E A L Y N J D Z C
I U L O M Q S C D Z R V D B V
H U O G F O J M G M C M R A I
P K H A T E G N D G B W H H B
```

Asia has so much variety in its many lands and waters. From tall snow-capped mountains, to hot and dry deserts, lush jungles to treeless tundra. Can you find these regions in the puzzle?

HIMALAYAS, GOBI DESERT, SEA OF JAPAN, SEA OF OKHOTSK, SOUTH CHINA SEA, BAY OF BENGAL, PHILIPPINE SEA, CASPIAN SEA

URAL MOUNTAINS

CENTRAL ASIA STEPPES

CASPIAN SEA

Unlike their African cousins, Asian elephants have been a big part of the work and cultural life of many nations.

Mount Everest is found in the Himalayan mountain range in the country of Nepal, along its border with China. It is the tallest point on land, reaching a height of 29,029 feet.

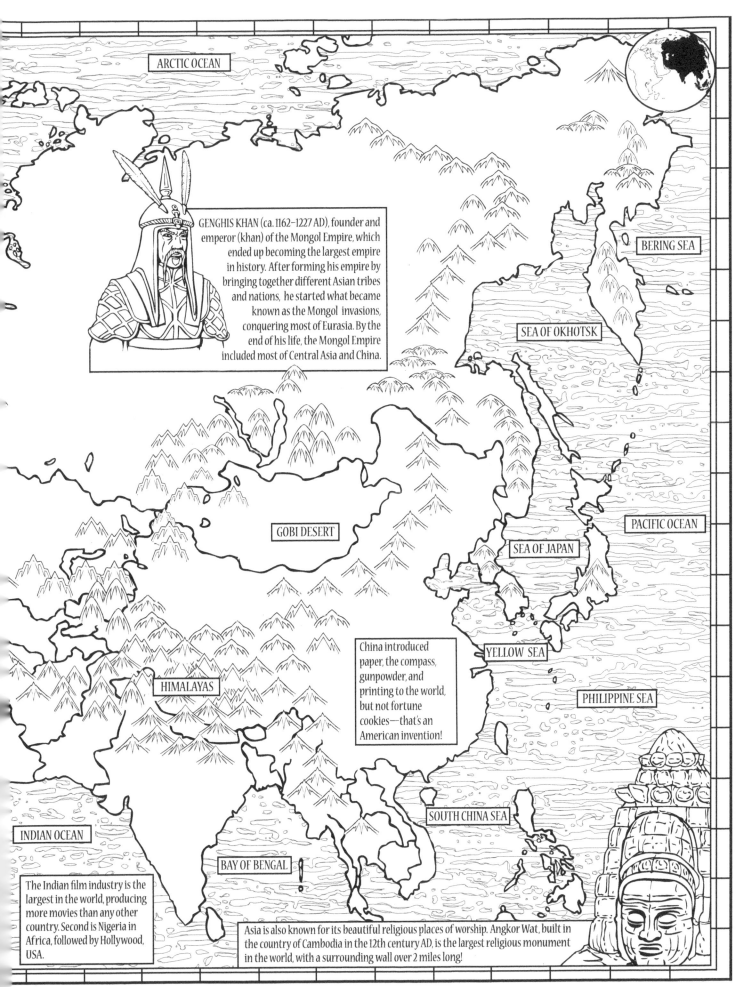

ARCTIC OCEAN

BERING SEA

SEA OF OKHOTSK

GENGHIS KHAN (ca. 1162–1227 AD), founder and emperor (khan) of the Mongol Empire, which ended up becoming the largest empire in history. After forming his empire by bringing together different Asian tribes and nations, he started what became known as the Mongol invasions, conquering most of Eurasia. By the end of his life, the Mongol Empire included most of Central Asia and China.

PACIFIC OCEAN

GOBI DESERT

SEA OF JAPAN

China introduced paper, the compass, gunpowder, and printing to the world, but not fortune cookies—that's an American invention!

YELLOW SEA

HIMALAYAS

PHILIPPINE SEA

SOUTH CHINA SEA

INDIAN OCEAN

BAY OF BENGAL

The Indian film industry is the largest in the world, producing more movies than any other country. Second is Nigeria in Africa, followed by Hollywood, USA.

Asia is also known for its beautiful religious places of worship. Angkor Wat, built in the country of Cambodia in the 12th century AD, is the largest religious monument in the world, with a surrounding wall over 2 miles long!

Like other ancient cultures, Indian scholars and religious leaders had a fascination with the movements of stars and planets. They realized the value of astronomy, and so they built large, complex observatories to help them study the stars with great accuracy. This made it possible for them to develop calendars and keep time through the year.

The cobra has been a part of Indian legend and culture. Here's your opportunity to draw one of these awesome creatures. The grid over the drawing of the cobra is the same as the large space above.

INDIAN OCEAN

Jantar Mantar Observatory

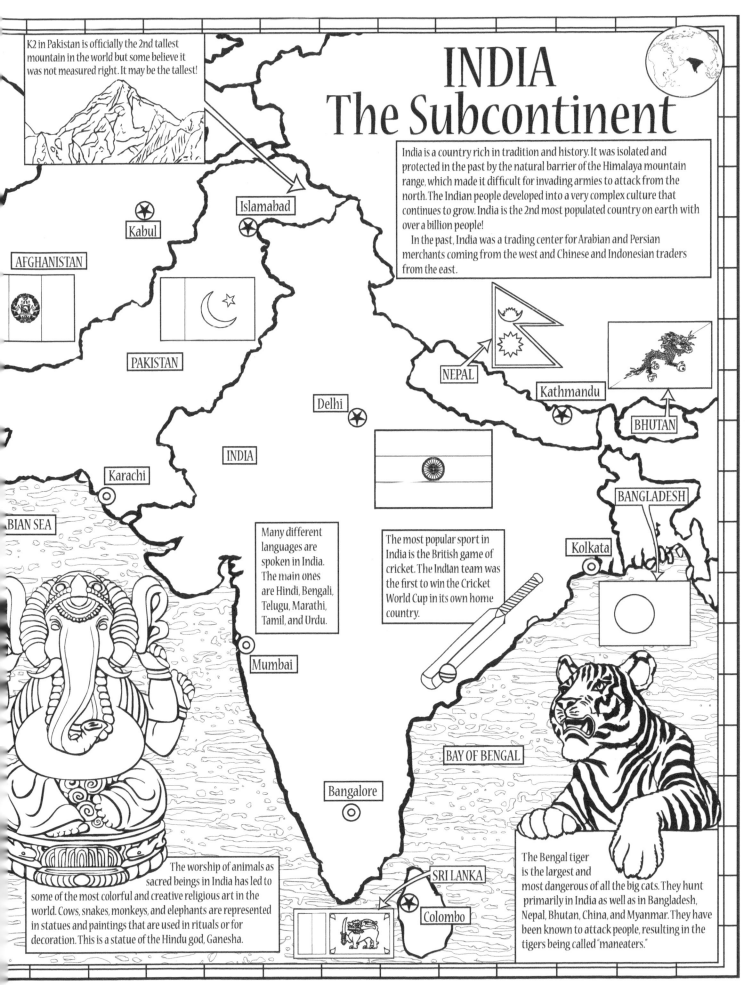

INDIA
The Subcontinent

India is a country rich in tradition and history. It was isolated and protected in the past by the natural barrier of the Himalaya mountain range, which made it difficult for invading armies to attack from the north. The Indian people developed into a very complex culture that continues to grow. India is the 2nd most populated country on earth with over a billion people!

In the past, India was a trading center for Arabian and Persian merchants coming from the west and Chinese and Indonesian traders from the east.

K2 in Pakistan is officially the 2nd tallest mountain in the world but some believe it was not measured right. It may be the tallest!

Kabul

AFGHANISTAN

Islamabad

PAKISTAN

NEPAL

Kathmandu

BHUTAN

Delhi

INDIA

BANGLADESH

Karachi

BIAN SEA

Kolkata

Many different languages are spoken in India. The main ones are Hindi, Bengali, Telugu, Marathi, Tamil, and Urdu.

The most popular sport in India is the British game of cricket. The Indian team was the first to win the Cricket World Cup in its own home country.

Mumbai

BAY OF BENGAL

Bangalore

The worship of animals as sacred beings in India has led to some of the most colorful and creative religious art in the world. Cows, snakes, monkeys, and elephants are represented in statues and paintings that are used in rituals or for decoration. This is a statue of the Hindu god, Ganesha.

SRI LANKA

Colombo

The Bengal tiger is the largest and most dangerous of all the big cats. They hunt primarily in India as well as in Bangladesh, Nepal, Bhutan, China, and Myanmar. They have been known to attack people, resulting in the tigers being called "maneaters."

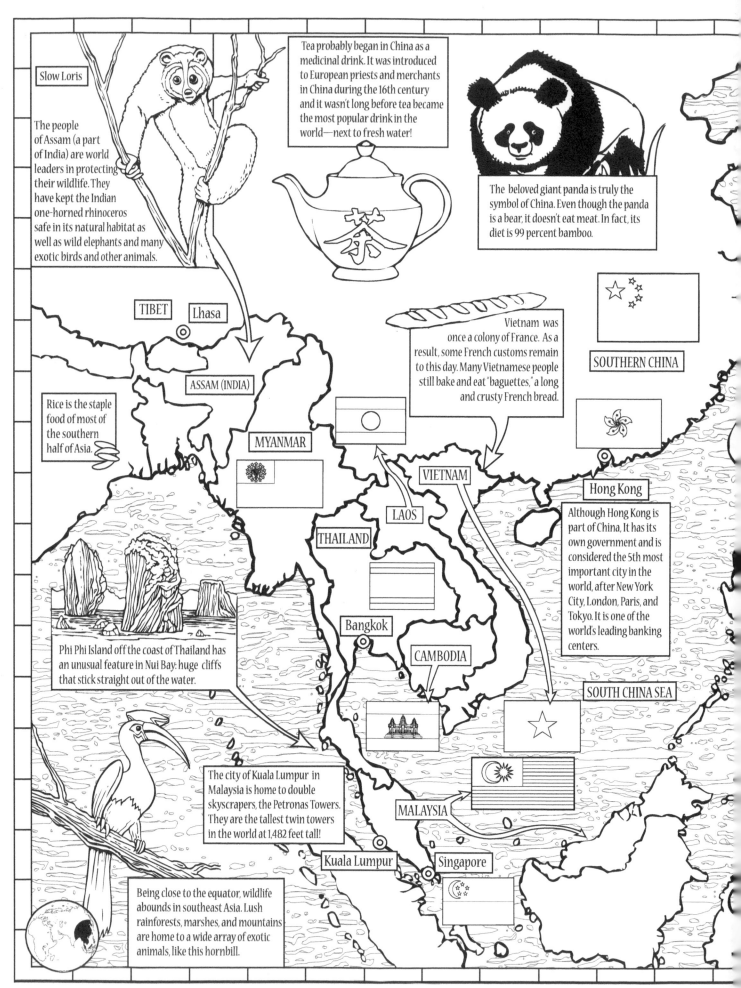

Slow Loris

The people of Assam (a part of India) are world leaders in protecting their wildlife. They have kept the Indian one-horned rhinoceros safe in its natural habitat as well as wild elephants and many exotic birds and other animals.

Tea probably began in China as a medicinal drink. It was introduced to European priests and merchants in China during the 16th century and it wasn't long before tea became the most popular drink in the world—next to fresh water!

The beloved giant panda is truly the symbol of China. Even though the panda is a bear, it doesn't eat meat. In fact, its diet is 99 percent bamboo.

TIBET   Lhasa ◎

ASSAM (INDIA)

Rice is the staple food of most of the southern half of Asia.

MYANMAR

SOUTHERN CHINA

Vietnam was once a colony of France. As a result, some French customs remain to this day. Many Vietnamese people still bake and eat "baguettes," a long and crusty French bread.

VIETNAM

LAOS

THAILAND

Hong Kong ◎

Although Hong Kong is part of China, It has its own government and is considered the 5th most important city in the world, after New York City, London, Paris, and Tokyo. It is one of the world's leading banking centers.

Bangkok ◎

CAMBODIA

Phi Phi Island off the coast of Thailand has an unusual feature in Nui Bay: huge cliffs that stick straight out of the water.

SOUTH CHINA SEA

The city of Kuala Lumpur in Malaysia is home to double skyscrapers, the Petronas Towers. They are the tallest twin towers in the world at 1,482 feet tall!

MALAYSIA

Kuala Lumpur ◎   Singapore ◎

Being close to the equator, wildlife abounds in southeast Asia. Lush rainforests, marshes, and mountains are home to a wide array of exotic animals, like this hornbill.

SOUTHEAST ASIA

Southeast Asia consists of 11 countries that are south of China, east of India, west of New Guinea and north of Australia. It is divided into two sub-regions: mainland southeast Asia (formerly called Indochina) and maritime southeast Asia (including Indonesia and the Philippines).

NORTH KOREA

SEA OF JAPAN

Seoul

SOUTH KOREA

Shanghai

EAST CHINA SEA

TAIWAN

PACIFIC OCEAN

PHILIPPINE SEA

There are many large temples and statues in southeast Asia that are visited by millions of people every year. This gigantic statue of a reclining Buddha is found in the country of Laos. Can you make your way up the hill?

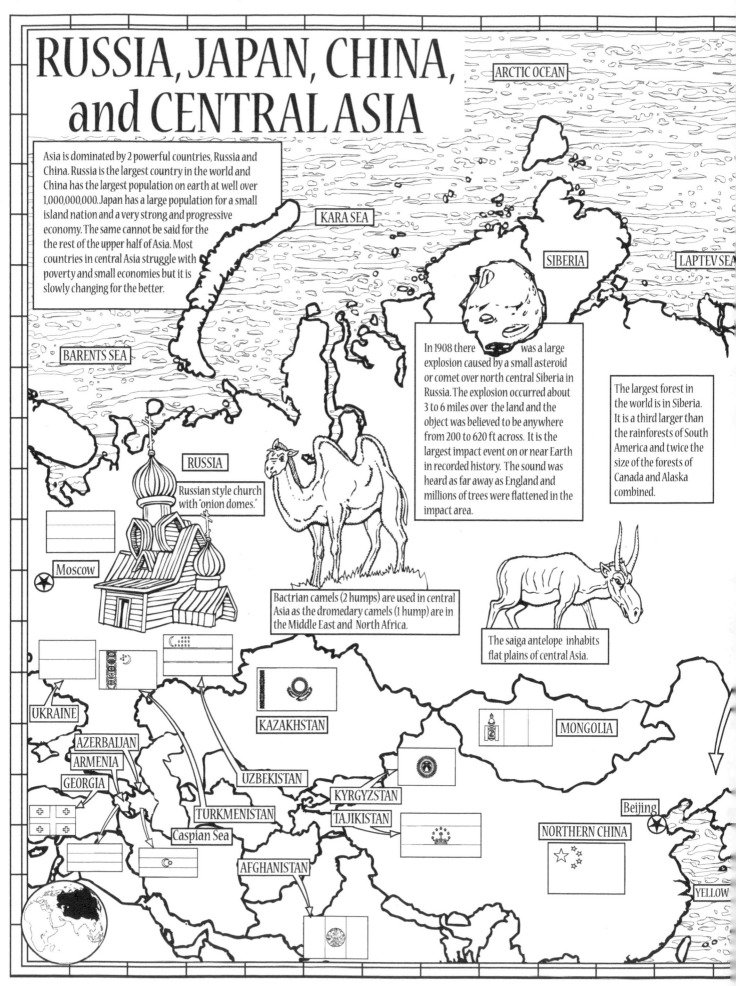

RUSSIA, JAPAN, CHINA, and CENTRAL ASIA

Asia is dominated by 2 powerful countries, Russia and China. Russia is the largest country in the world and China has the largest population on earth at well over 1,000,000,000. Japan has a large population for a small island nation and a very strong and progressive economy. The same cannot be said for the the rest of the upper half of Asia. Most countries in central Asia struggle with poverty and small economies but it is slowly changing for the better.

ARCTIC OCEAN

KARA SEA

SIBERIA

LAPTEV SEA

BARENTS SEA

RUSSIA

Russian style church with "onion domes."

In 1908 there was a large explosion caused by a small asteroid or comet over north central Siberia in Russia. The explosion occurred about 3 to 6 miles over the land and the object was believed to be anywhere from 200 to 620 ft across. It is the largest impact event on or near Earth in recorded history. The sound was heard as far away as England and millions of trees were flattened in the impact area.

The largest forest in the world is in Siberia. It is a third larger than the rainforests of South America and twice the size of the forests of Canada and Alaska combined.

Moscow

Bactrian camels (2 humps) are used in central Asia as the dromedary camels (1 hump) are in the Middle East and North Africa.

The saiga antelope inhabits flat plains of central Asia.

UKRAINE

KAZAKHSTAN

MONGOLIA

AZERBAIJAN

ARMENIA

GEORGIA

UZBEKISTAN

KYRGYZSTAN

TURKMENISTAN

TAJIKISTAN

Beijing

Caspian Sea

NORTHERN CHINA

AFGHANISTAN

YELLOW

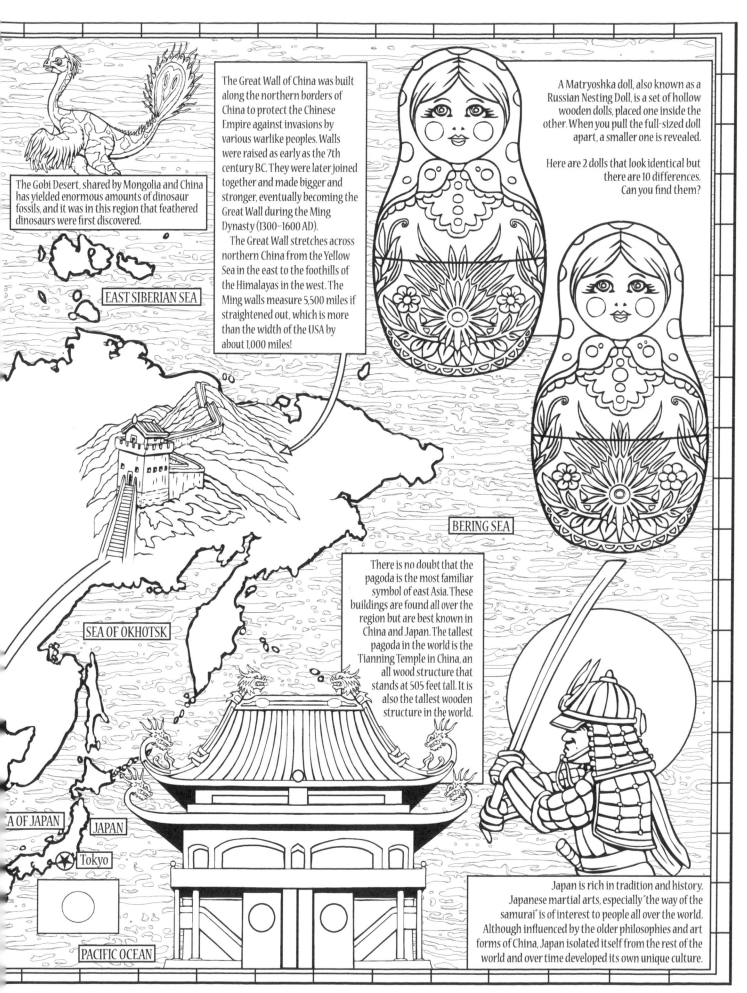

The Gobi Desert, shared by Mongolia and China has yielded enormous amounts of dinosaur fossils, and it was in this region that feathered dinosaurs were first discovered.

The Great Wall of China was built along the northern borders of China to protect the Chinese Empire against invasions by various warlike peoples. Walls were raised as early as the 7th century BC. They were later joined together and made bigger and stronger, eventually becoming the Great Wall during the Ming Dynasty (1300–1600 AD).

The Great Wall stretches across northern China from the Yellow Sea in the east to the foothills of the Himalayas in the west. The Ming walls measure 5,500 miles if straightened out, which is more than the width of the USA by about 1,000 miles!

A Matryoshka doll, also known as a Russian Nesting Doll, is a set of hollow wooden dolls, placed one inside the other. When you pull the full-sized doll apart, a smaller one is revealed.

Here are 2 dolls that look identical but there are 10 differences. Can you find them?

EAST SIBERIAN SEA

BERING SEA

SEA OF OKHOTSK

There is no doubt that the pagoda is the most familiar symbol of east Asia. These buildings are found all over the region but are best known in China and Japan. The tallest pagoda in the world is the Tianning Temple in China, an all wood structure that stands at 505 feet tall. It is also the tallest wooden structure in the world.

A OF JAPAN

JAPAN

Tokyo

PACIFIC OCEAN

Japan is rich in tradition and history. Japanese martial arts, especially "the way of the samurai" is of interest to people all over the world. Although influenced by the older philosophies and art forms of China, Japan isolated itself from the rest of the world and over time developed its own unique culture.

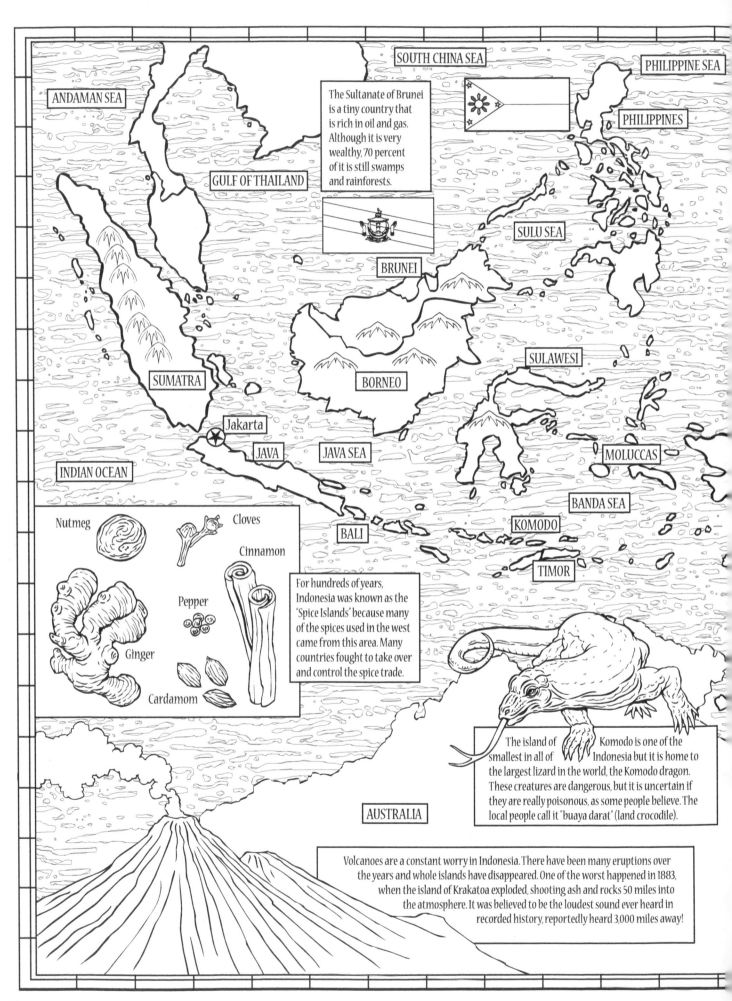

ANDAMAN SEA

SOUTH CHINA SEA

PHILIPPINE SEA

The Sultanate of Brunei is a tiny country that is rich in oil and gas. Although it is very wealthy, 70 percent of it is still swamps and rainforests.

GULF OF THAILAND

PHILIPPINES

SULU SEA

BRUNEI

SUMATRA

BORNEO

SULAWESI

Jakarta

JAVA

JAVA SEA

MOLUCCAS

INDIAN OCEAN

BANDA SEA

BALI

KOMODO

TIMOR

Nutmeg

Cloves

Cinnamon

Pepper

Ginger

Cardamom

For hundreds of years, Indonesia was known as the "Spice Islands" because many of the spices used in the west came from this area. Many countries fought to take over and control the spice trade.

The island of Komodo is one of the smallest in all of Indonesia but it is home to the largest lizard in the world, the Komodo dragon. These creatures are dangerous, but it is uncertain if they are really poisonous, as some people believe. The local people call it "buaya darat" (land crocodile).

AUSTRALIA

Volcanoes are a constant worry in Indonesia. There have been many eruptions over the years and whole islands have disappeared. One of the worst happened in 1883, when the island of Krakatoa exploded, shooting ash and rocks 50 miles into the atmosphere. It was believed to be the loudest sound ever heard in recorded history, reportedly heard 3,000 miles away!

INDONESIA
Major Islands

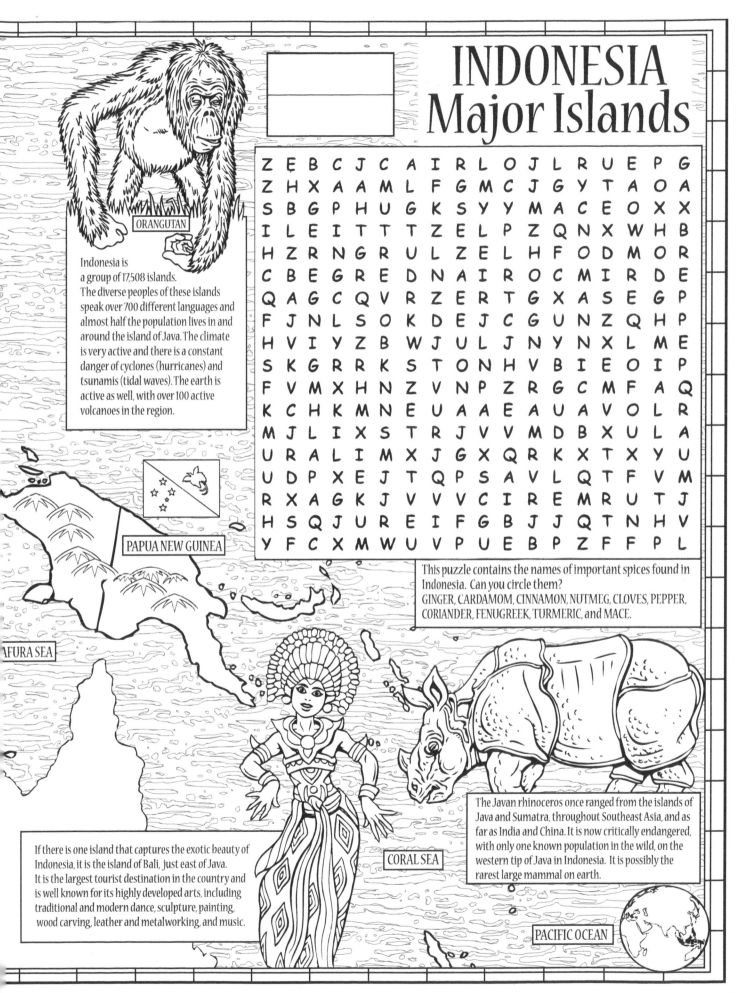

ORANGUTAN

Indonesia is a group of 17,508 islands. The diverse peoples of these islands speak over 700 different languages and almost half the population lives in and around the island of Java. The climate is very active and there is a constant danger of cyclones (hurricanes) and tsunamis (tidal waves). The earth is active as well, with over 100 active volcanoes in the region.

```
Z E B C J C A I R L O J L R U E P G
Z H X A A M L F G M C J G Y T A O A
S B G P H U G K S Y Y M A C E O X X
I L E I T T Z E L P Z Q N X W H B
H Z R N G R U L Z E L H F O D M O R
C B E G R E D N A I R O C M I R D E
Q A G C Q V R Z E R T G X A S E G P
F J N L S O K D E J C G U N Z Q H P
H V I Y Z B W J U L J N Y N X L M E
S K G R R K S T O N H V B I E O I P
F V M X H N Z V N P Z R G C M F A Q
K C H K M N E U A A E A U A V O L R
M J L I X S T R J V V M D B X U L A
U R A L I M X J G X Q R K X T X Y U
U D P X E J T Q P S A V L Q T F Y M
R X A G K J V V V C I R E M R U T J
H S Q J U R E I F G B J J Q T N H V
Y F C X M W U V P U E B P Z F F P L
```

PAPUA NEW GUINEA

This puzzle contains the names of important spices found in Indonesia. Can you circle them?
GINGER, CARDAMOM, CINNAMON, NUTMEG, CLOVES, PEPPER, CORIANDER, FENUGREEK, TURMERIC, and MACE.

AFURA SEA

If there is one island that captures the exotic beauty of Indonesia, it is the island of Bali, just east of Java. It is the largest tourist destination in the country and is well known for its highly developed arts, including traditional and modern dance, sculpture, painting, wood carving, leather and metalworking, and music.

CORAL SEA

The Javan rhinoceros once ranged from the islands of Java and Sumatra, throughout Southeast Asia, and as far as India and China. It is now critically endangered, with only one known population in the wild, on the western tip of Java in Indonesia. It is possibly the rarest large mammal on earth.

PACIFIC OCEAN

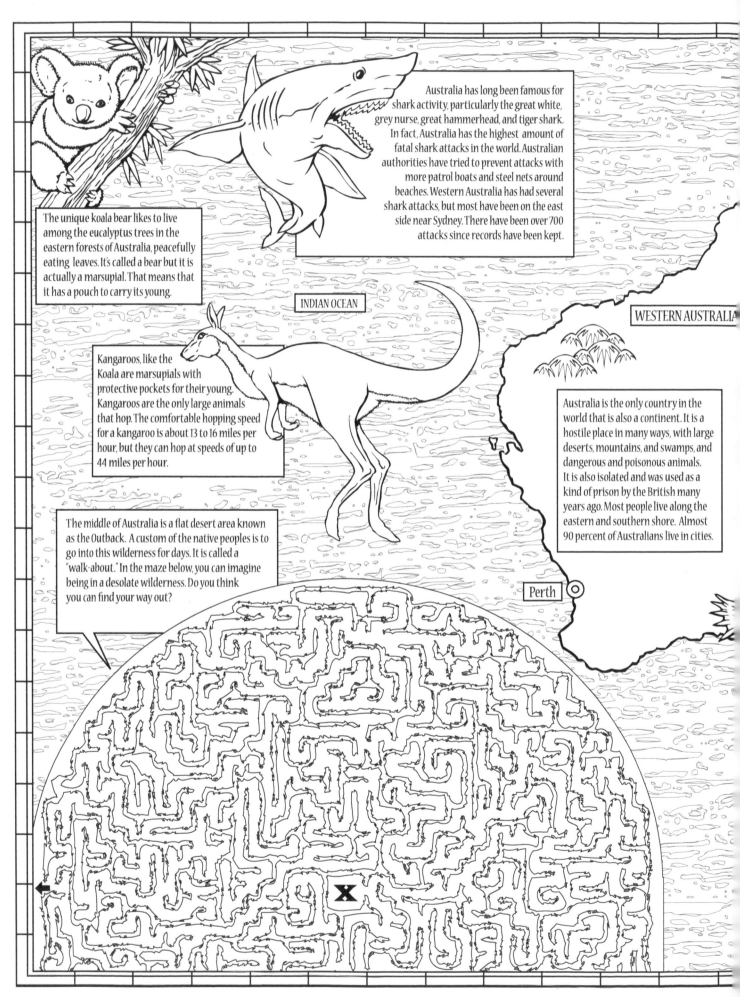

Australia has long been famous for shark activity, particularly the great white, grey nurse, great hammerhead, and tiger shark. In fact, Australia has the highest amount of fatal shark attacks in the world. Australian authorities have tried to prevent attacks with more patrol boats and steel nets around beaches. Western Australia has had several shark attacks, but most have been on the east side near Sydney. There have been over 700 attacks since records have been kept.

The unique koala bear likes to live among the eucalyptus trees in the eastern forests of Australia, peacefully eating leaves. It's called a bear but it is actually a marsupial. That means that it has a pouch to carry its young.

INDIAN OCEAN

WESTERN AUSTRALIA

Kangaroos, like the Koala are marsupials with protective pockets for their young. Kangaroos are the only large animals that hop. The comfortable hopping speed for a kangaroo is about 13 to 16 miles per hour, but they can hop at speeds of up to 44 miles per hour.

Australia is the only country in the world that is also a continent. It is a hostile place in many ways, with large deserts, mountains, and swamps, and dangerous and poisonous animals. It is also isolated and was used as a kind of prison by the British many years ago. Most people live along the eastern and southern shore. Almost 90 percent of Australians live in cities.

The middle of Australia is a flat desert area known as the Outback. A custom of the native peoples is to go into this wilderness for days. It is called a "walk-about." In the maze below, you can imagine being in a desolate wilderness. Do you think you can find your way out?

Perth

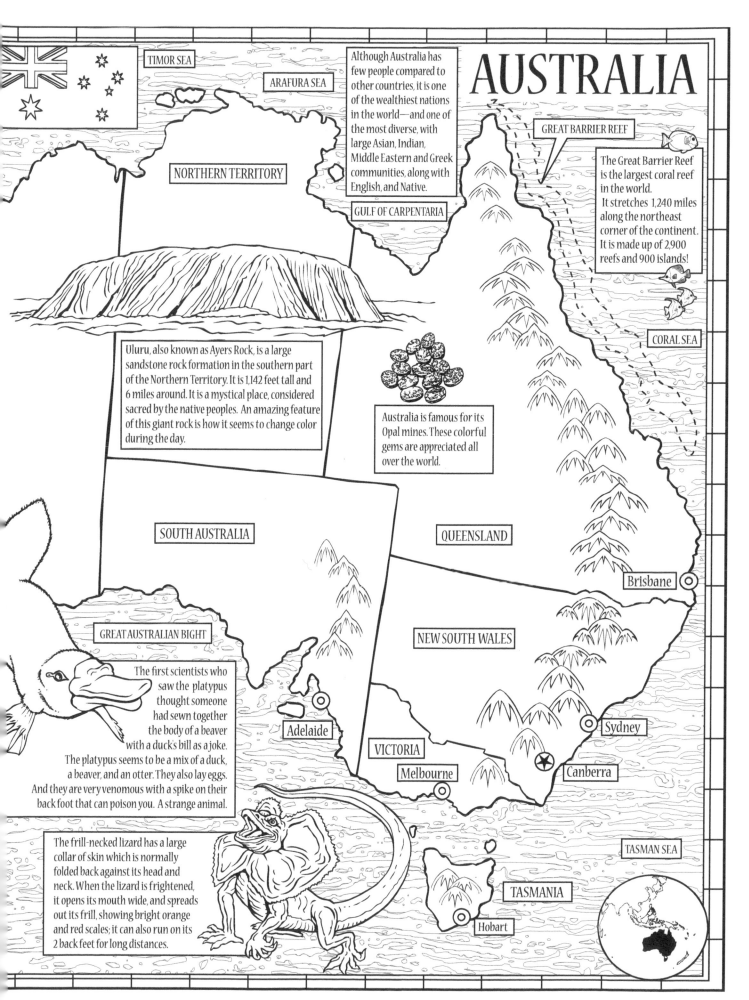

AUSTRALIA

TIMOR SEA

ARAFURA SEA

NORTHERN TERRITORY

GULF OF CARPENTARIA

Although Australia has few people compared to other countries, it is one of the wealthiest nations in the world—and one of the most diverse, with large Asian, Indian, Middle Eastern and Greek communities, along with English, and Native.

GREAT BARRIER REEF

The Great Barrier Reef is the largest coral reef in the world.
It stretches 1,240 miles along the northeast corner of the continent. It is made up of 2,900 reefs and 900 islands!

CORAL SEA

Uluru, also known as Ayers Rock, is a large sandstone rock formation in the southern part of the Northern Territory. It is 1,142 feet tall and 6 miles around. It is a mystical place, considered sacred by the native peoples. An amazing feature of this giant rock is how it seems to change color during the day.

Australia is famous for its Opal mines. These colorful gems are appreciated all over the world.

SOUTH AUSTRALIA

QUEENSLAND

Brisbane

GREAT AUSTRALIAN BIGHT

NEW SOUTH WALES

The first scientists who saw the platypus thought someone had sewn together the body of a beaver with a duck's bill as a joke. The platypus seems to be a mix of a duck, a beaver, and an otter. They also lay eggs. And they are very venomous with a spike on their back foot that can poison you. A strange animal.

Adelaide

VICTORIA

Melbourne

Sydney

Canberra

The frill-necked lizard has a large collar of skin which is normally folded back against its head and neck. When the lizard is frightened, it opens its mouth wide, and spreads out its frill, showing bright orange and red scales; it can also run on its 2 back feet for long distances.

TASMAN SEA

TASMANIA

Hobart

49

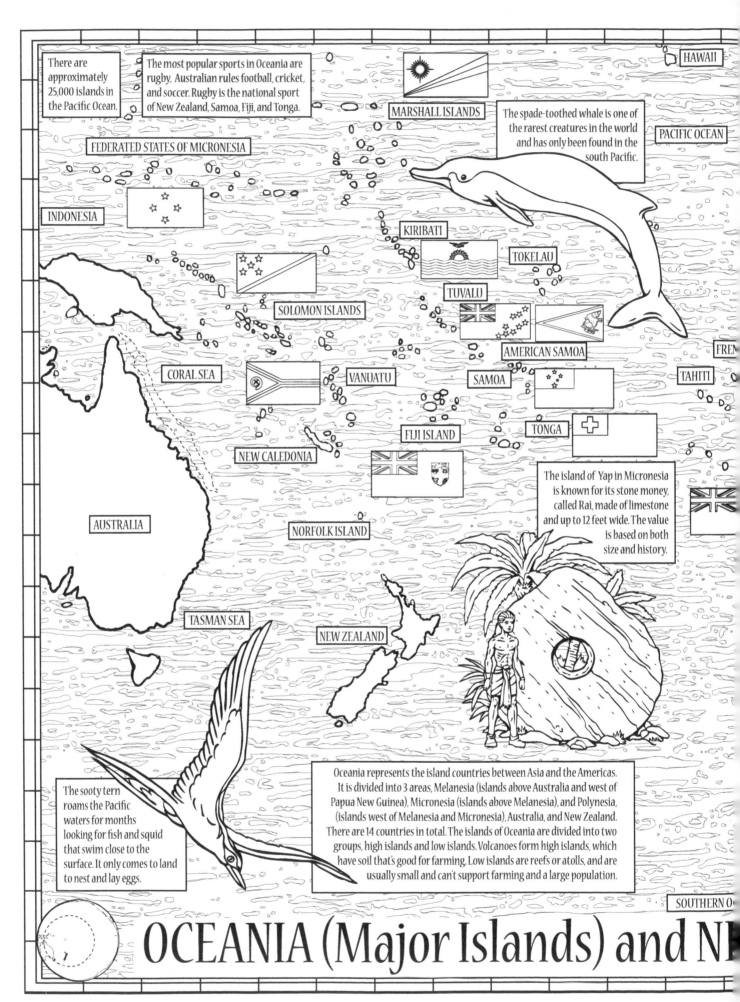

There are approximately 25,000 islands in the Pacific Ocean.

The most popular sports in Oceania are rugby, Australian rules football, cricket, and soccer. Rugby is the national sport of New Zealand, Samoa, Fiji, and Tonga.

HAWAII

MARSHALL ISLANDS

The spade-toothed whale is one of the rarest creatures in the world and has only been found in the south Pacific.

PACIFIC OCEAN

FEDERATED STATES OF MICRONESIA

INDONESIA

KIRIBATI

TOKELAU

TUVALU

SOLOMON ISLANDS

AMERICAN SAMOA

FREM

CORAL SEA

VANUATU

SAMOA

TAHITI

TONGA

FIJI ISLAND

The island of Yap in Micronesia is known for its stone money, called Rai, made of limestone and up to 12 feet wide. The value is based on both size and history.

NEW CALEDONIA

AUSTRALIA

NORFOLK ISLAND

TASMAN SEA

NEW ZEALAND

The sooty tern roams the Pacific waters for months looking for fish and squid that swim close to the surface. It only comes to land to nest and lay eggs.

Oceania represents the island countries between Asia and the Americas. It is divided into 3 areas, Melanesia (islands above Australia and west of Papua New Guinea), Micronesia (islands above Melanesia), and Polynesia, (islands west of Melanesia and Micronesia), Australia, and New Zealand. There are 14 countries in total. The islands of Oceania are divided into two groups, high islands and low islands. Volcanoes form high islands, which have soil that's good for farming. Low islands are reefs or atolls, and are usually small and can't support farming and a large population.

SOUTHERN O

OCEANIA (Major Islands) and NI

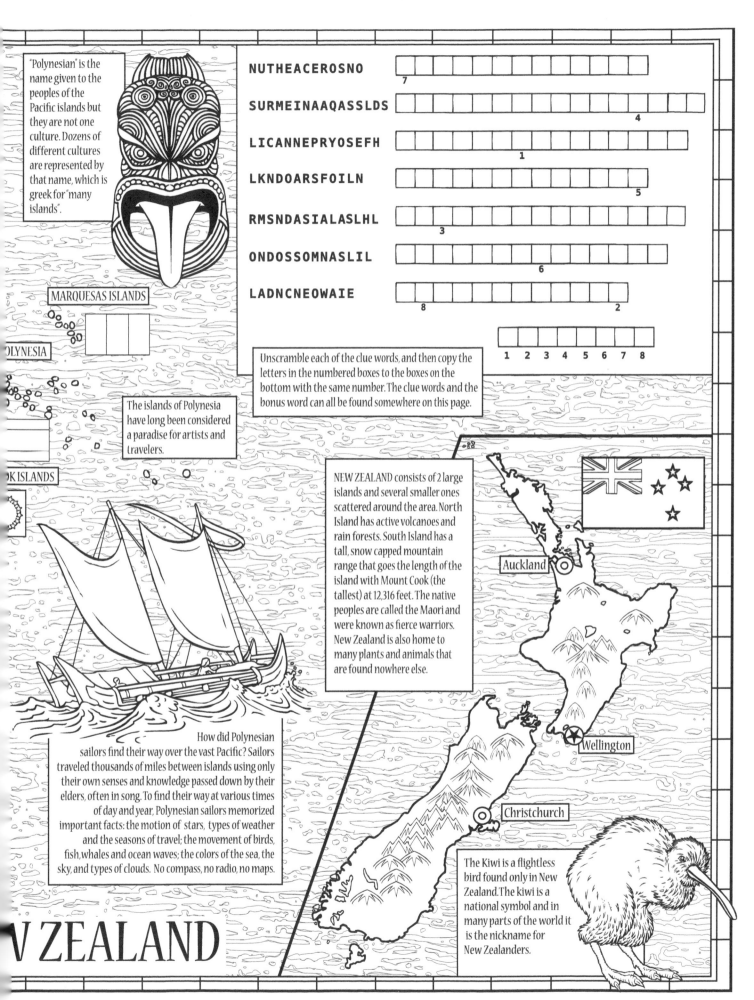

"Polynesian" is the name given to the peoples of the Pacific islands but they are not one culture. Dozens of different cultures are represented by that name, which is greek for "many islands".

MARQUESAS ISLANDS

POLYNESIA

COOK ISLANDS

The islands of Polynesia have long been considered a paradise for artists and travelers.

NUTHEACEROSNO

SURMEINAAQASSLDS

LICANNEPRYOSEFH

LKNDOARSFOILN

RMSNDASIALASLHL

ONDOSSOMNASLIL

LADNCNEOWAIE

1 2 3 4 5 6 7 8

Unscramble each of the clue words, and then copy the letters in the numbered boxes to the boxes on the bottom with the same number. The clue words and the bonus word can all be found somewhere on this page.

NEW ZEALAND consists of 2 large islands and several smaller ones scattered around the area. North Island has active volcanoes and rain forests. South Island has a tall, snow capped mountain range that goes the length of the island with Mount Cook (the tallest) at 12,316 feet. The native peoples are called the Maori and were known as fierce warriors. New Zealand is also home to many plants and animals that are found nowhere else.

Auckland

Wellington

Christchurch

How did Polynesian sailors find their way over the vast Pacific? Sailors traveled thousands of miles between islands using only their own senses and knowledge passed down by their elders, often in song. To find their way at various times of day and year, Polynesian sailors memorized important facts: the motion of stars, types of weather and the seasons of travel; the movement of birds, fish, whales and ocean waves; the colors of the sea, the sky, and types of clouds. No compass, no radio, no maps.

V ZEALAND

The Kiwi is a flightless bird found only in New Zealand. The kiwi is a national symbol and in many parts of the world it is the nickname for New Zealanders.

AFRICA

There is a reason why Africa was known for centuries as the "Dark Continent": It was difficult to get into the interior. People had been living on the north shore but there were so many natural obstacles preventing any further entry. The Atlas mountains stood in the way along the northwest, followed by a massive desert that took up the whole top half. The land then changes to miles and miles of desolate grasslands, then into deep, dense jungle. Not very hospitable!

There are over 2,000 distinct languages spoken in Africa, and many countries even have national sign languages.

ACROSS
3. SOMETHING IN YOUR WAY
5. WHAT AN ANIMAL FACES WHEN IT'S IN DANGER OF DISAPPEARING
8. BODY OF WATER ON THE NORTH SHORE
9. A LAKE IN EAST-CENTRAL AFRICA

All the words in this puzzle are on these 2 pages.

ATLANTIC O

DOWN
1. IF YOU HAVE A POPULATION OF MORE THAN 10,000,000 PEOPLE, YOU HAVE ONE OF THESE
2. YOU CAN'T MAKE CHOCOLATE WITHOUT THESE
4. YOU NEED THIS TO MAKE GASOLINE
6. LIKE A PONY WITH STRIPES
7. THE LONGEST RIVER ON EARTH

One of Africa's most interesting features is actually its wildlife. Zebras, giraffes, lions, rhinos, hippos, and great apes amazed people in Europe and Asia when they first saw them. They were collected by wealthy people in what were called "menageries" (later to become public zoos) and the ancient Romans even used them for entertainment in their colosseum and arena games. Early merchants and explorers were awe-struck by the huge numbers of animals traveling in herds across the landscape, the unusual trees and plants and the many dangerous insects and reptiles. Their numbers have gone down over the years and some animals are even in danger of extinction.

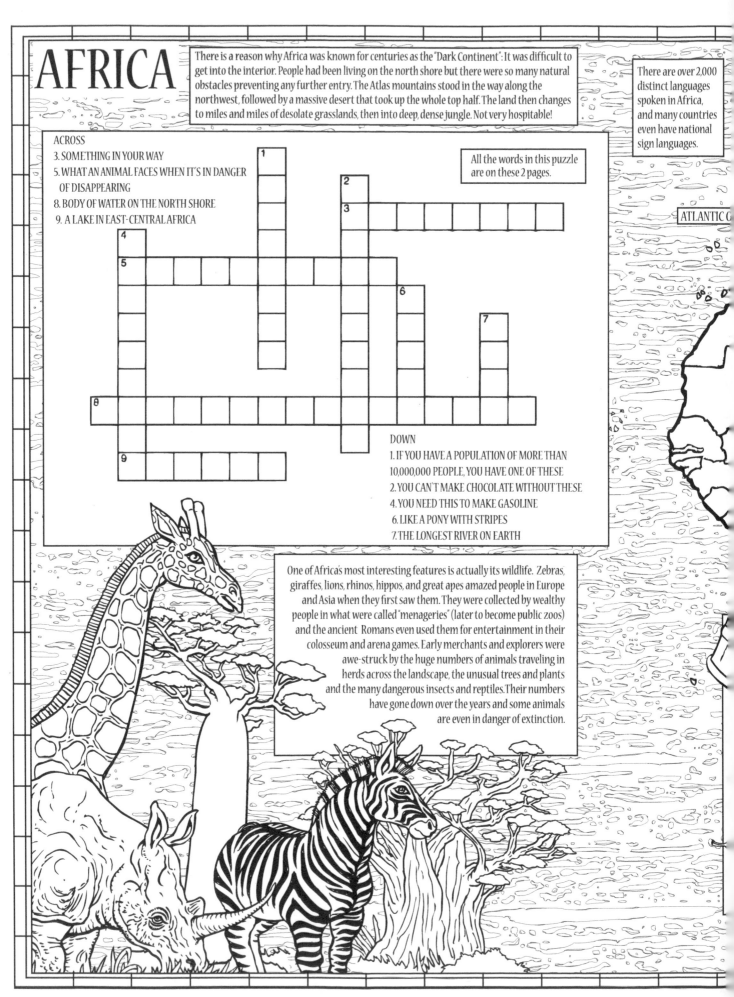

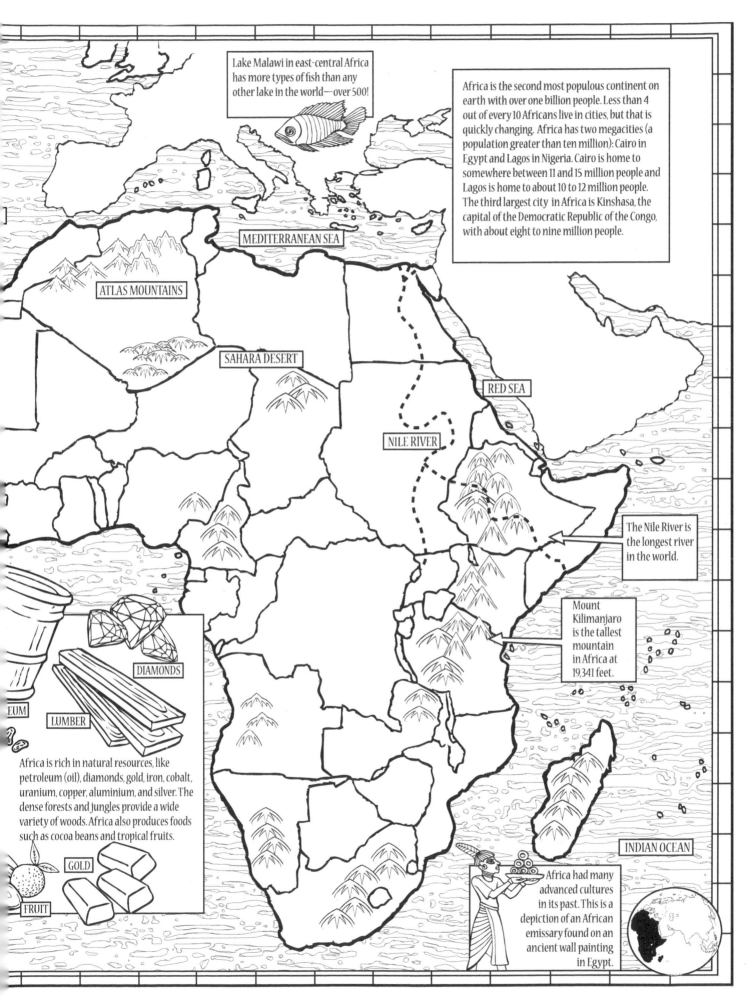

Lake Malawi in east-central Africa has more types of fish than any other lake in the world—over 500!

Africa is the second most populous continent on earth with over one billion people. Less than 4 out of every 10 Africans live in cities, but that is quickly changing. Africa has two megacities (a population greater than ten million): Cairo in Egypt and Lagos in Nigeria. Cairo is home to somewhere between 11 and 15 million people and Lagos is home to about 10 to 12 million people. The third largest city in Africa is Kinshasa, the capital of the Democratic Republic of the Congo, with about eight to nine million people.

MEDITERRANEAN SEA

ATLAS MOUNTAINS

SAHARA DESERT

RED SEA

NILE RIVER

The Nile River is the longest river in the world.

Mount Kilimanjaro is the tallest mountain in Africa at 19,341 feet.

DIAMONDS

EUM

LUMBER

Africa is rich in natural resources, like petroleum (oil), diamonds, gold, iron, cobalt, uranium, copper, aluminium, and silver. The dense forests and jungles provide a wide variety of woods. Africa also produces foods such as cocoa beans and tropical fruits.

GOLD

FRUIT

INDIAN OCEAN

Africa had many advanced cultures in its past. This is a depiction of an African emissary found on an ancient wall painting in Egypt.

53

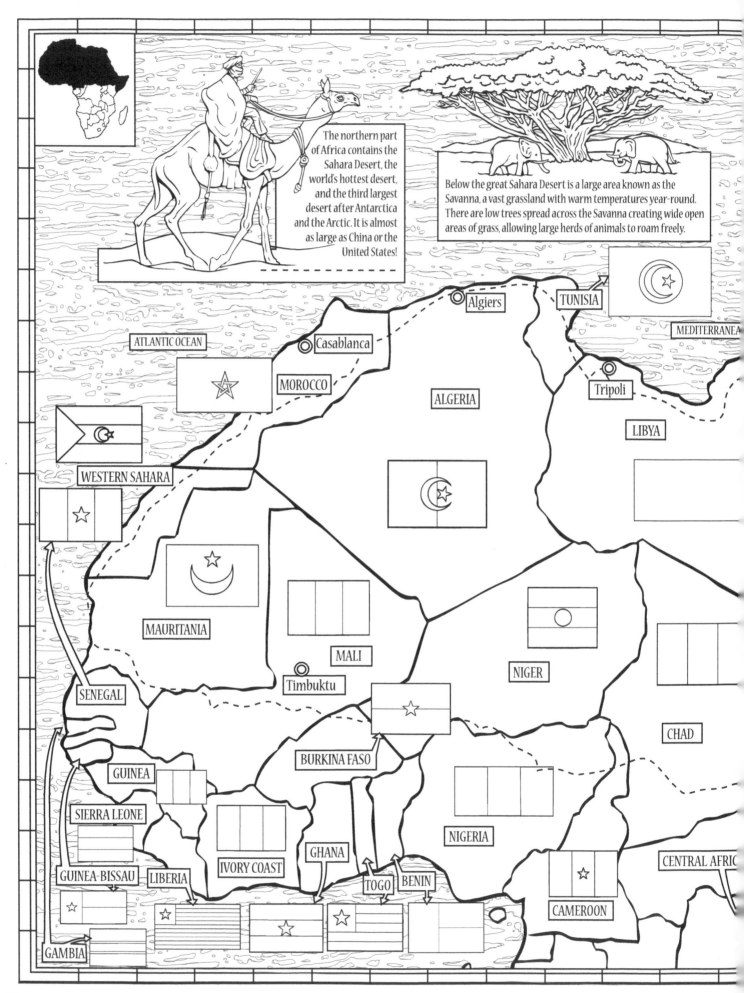

The northern part of Africa contains the Sahara Desert, the world's hottest desert, and the third largest desert after Antarctica and the Arctic. It is almost as large as China or the United States!

Below the great Sahara Desert is a large area known as the Savanna, a vast grassland with warm temperatures year-round. There are low trees spread across the Savanna creating wide open areas of grass, allowing large herds of animals to roam freely.

Algiers

TUNISIA

ATLANTIC OCEAN

Casablanca

MEDITERRANEA

MOROCCO

ALGERIA

Tripoli

LIBYA

WESTERN SAHARA

MAURITANIA

MALI

NIGER

Timbuktu

CHAD

SENEGAL

BURKINA FASO

GUINEA

SIERRA LEONE

NIGERIA

GHANA

CENTRAL AFRIC

GUINEA-BISSAU   LIBERIA   IVORY COAST

TOGO   BENIN

CAMEROON

GAMBIA

NORTHERN AFRICA (and Major Cities)

The greatest civilization of the ancient world was the Egyptian Empire, begun along the Nile river in the northeast corner of Africa more than 5,000 years ago.

Northern Africa is dominated by the Sahara Desert and so most people live on its outer edges, particularly along the Mediterranean coast where many civilizations rose and fell. The great Egyptian Empire, the Carthaginians, the Romans, the Byzantines, and ultimately, the Islamic peoples. Because of the natural barriers of mountains and desert, few people ventured south from the coast but there was continuous trade over the centuries between northern and central Africa for gold and other metals, precious stones, furs, ivory, and spices.

The use of coffee is thought to have started in Ethiopia in East Africa. Coffee brewing and drinking spread to the Middle East and then to Europe, becoming one of the most popular drinks in the world.

Africa is well known for its magnificent wood carvings, especially the ceremonial masks used in rituals. These 2 masks look identical but there are 10 differences. Can you find them?

One of Africa's greatest struggles is the protection of its unique animals from illegal hunters known as poachers. Many countries have enacted stricter laws to prevent the gradual disappearance of these beautiful creatures.

Cairo

EGYPT

RED SEA

SUDAN

ERITREA

DJIBOUTI

SOMALILAND

Addis Ababa

ETHIOPIA

SOMALIA

SOUTH SUDAN

EPUBLIC

Mogadishu

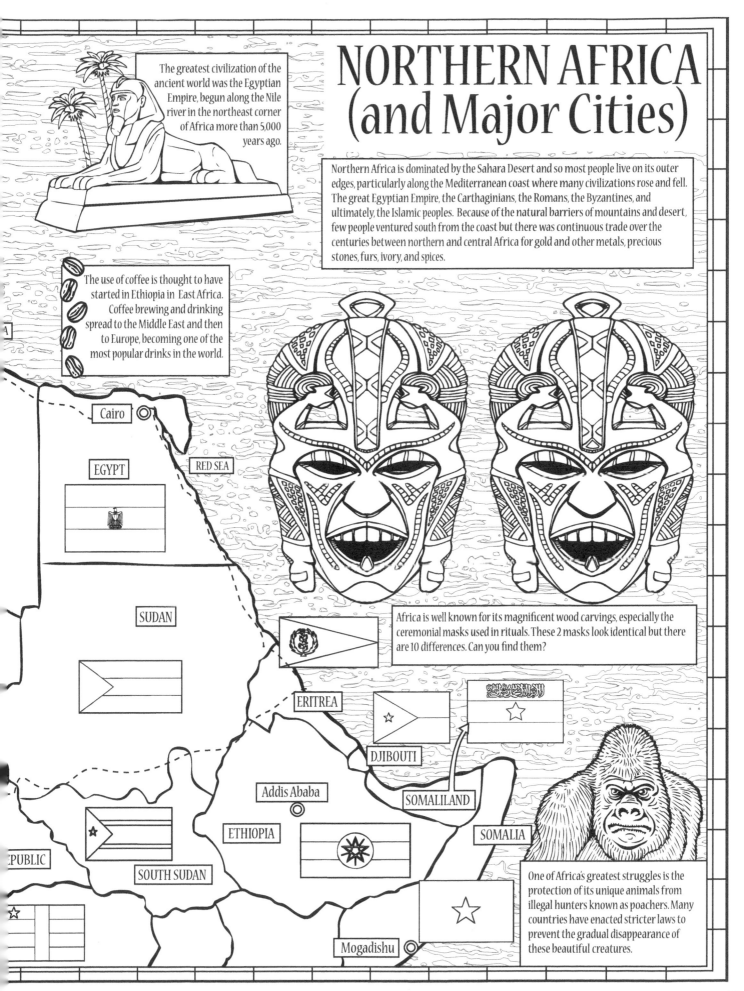

EQUATORIAL GUINEA

GABON

REPUBLIC OF CONGO

DEMOCRATIC REPUBLIC OF THE CONGO

Kinshasa

UGANDA

RWANDA

BURUNDI

KENYA

Nairobi

ANGOLA

ATLANTIC OCEAN

Zanzibar

TANZANIA

ZAMBIA

MALAWI

MOZAMBIQUE

NAMIBIA

ZIMBABWE

BOTSWANA

Johannesburg

SWAZILAND

The aardvark got its name
from 2 dutch words:
earth (aard) and pig (vark)
because it is an anteater
and digs into the ground.
Although not very big,
it is related to the elephant.

SOUTH AFRICA

LESOTHO

Cape Town

The hoopoe is
a bird found across
southern Africa
and Madagascar.
It gets its name
from the sound it makes.

Southern Africa has its
share of strange animals.
When local people spoke
of the okapi, an animal
that was part giraffe and
part zebra, they were
thought to be a myth—
until several were found
in the 19th century.

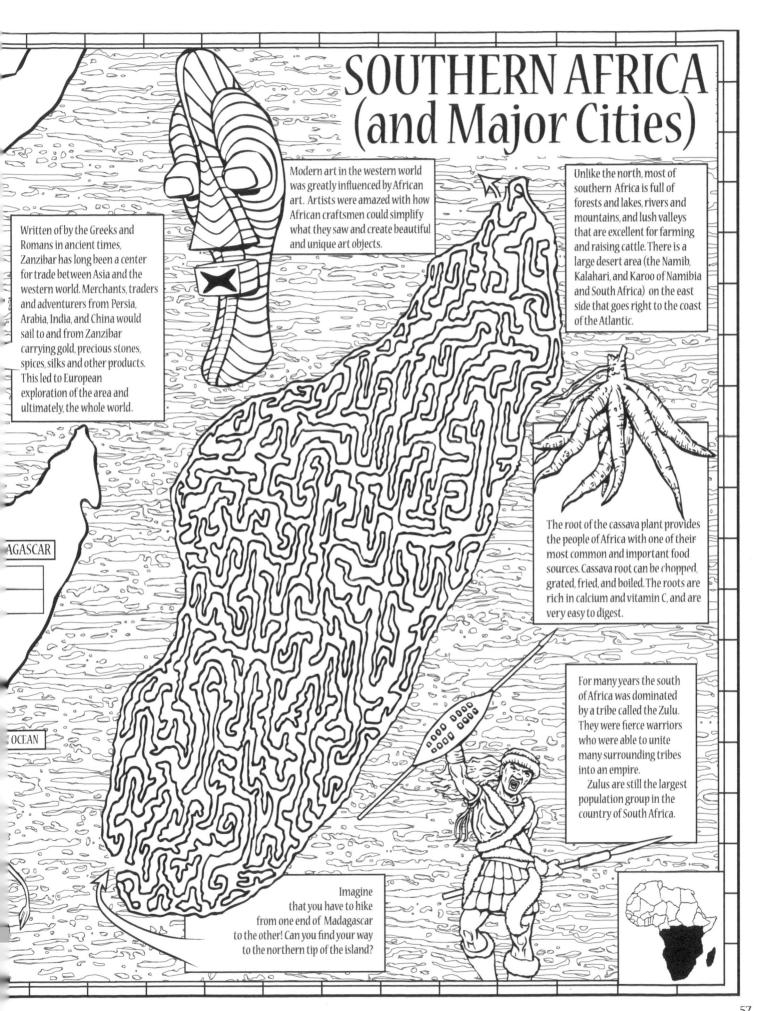

SOUTHERN AFRICA (and Major Cities)

Modern art in the western world was greatly influenced by African art. Artists were amazed with how African craftsmen could simplify what they saw and create beautiful and unique art objects.

Unlike the north, most of southern Africa is full of forests and lakes, rivers and mountains, and lush valleys that are excellent for farming and raising cattle. There is a large desert area (the Namib, Kalahari, and Karoo of Namibia and South Africa) on the east side that goes right to the coast of the Atlantic.

Written of by the Greeks and Romans in ancient times, Zanzibar has long been a center for trade between Asia and the western world. Merchants, traders and adventurers from Persia, Arabia, India, and China would sail to and from Zanzibar carrying gold, precious stones, spices, silks and other products. This led to European exploration of the area and ultimately, the whole world.

MAGASCAR

OCEAN

The root of the cassava plant provides the people of Africa with one of their most common and important food sources. Cassava root can be chopped, grated, fried, and boiled. The roots are rich in calcium and vitamin C, and are very easy to digest.

For many years the south of Africa was dominated by a tribe called the Zulu. They were fierce warriors who were able to unite many surrounding tribes into an empire.

Zulus are still the largest population group in the country of South Africa.

Imagine that you have to hike from one end of Madagascar to the other! Can you find your way to the northern tip of the island?

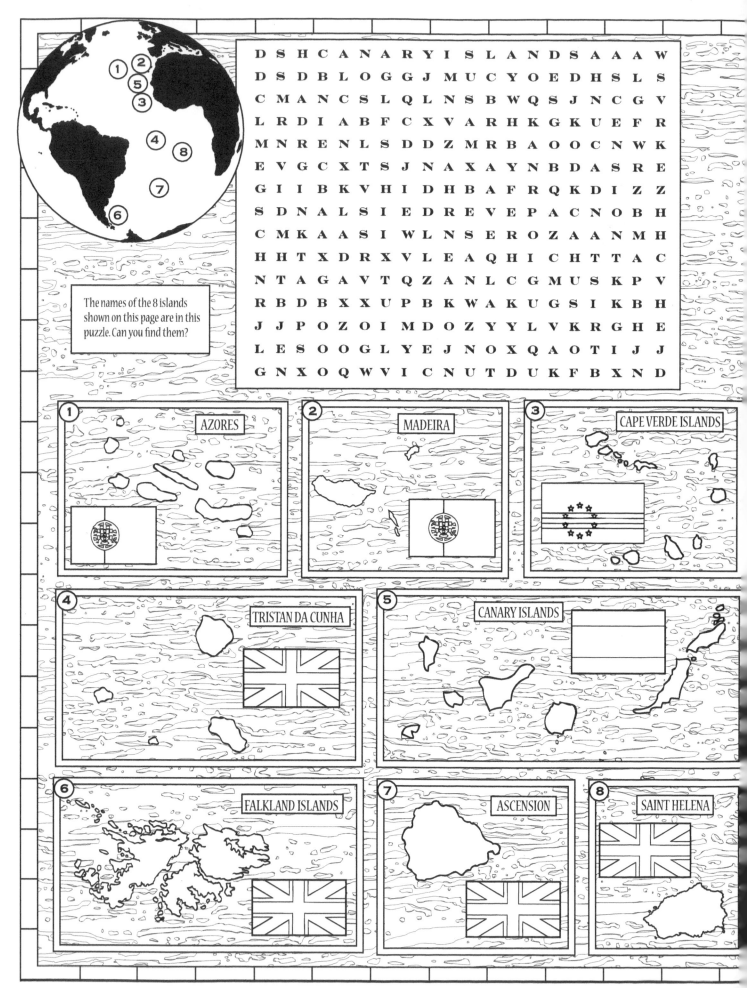

The names of the 8 islands shown on this page are in this puzzle. Can you find them?

1 AZORES
2 MADEIRA
3 CAPE VERDE ISLANDS
4 TRISTAN DA CUNHA
5 CANARY ISLANDS
6 FALKLAND ISLANDS
7 ASCENSION
8 SAINT HELENA

REMOTE ISLANDS
Atlantic and Pacific Oceans

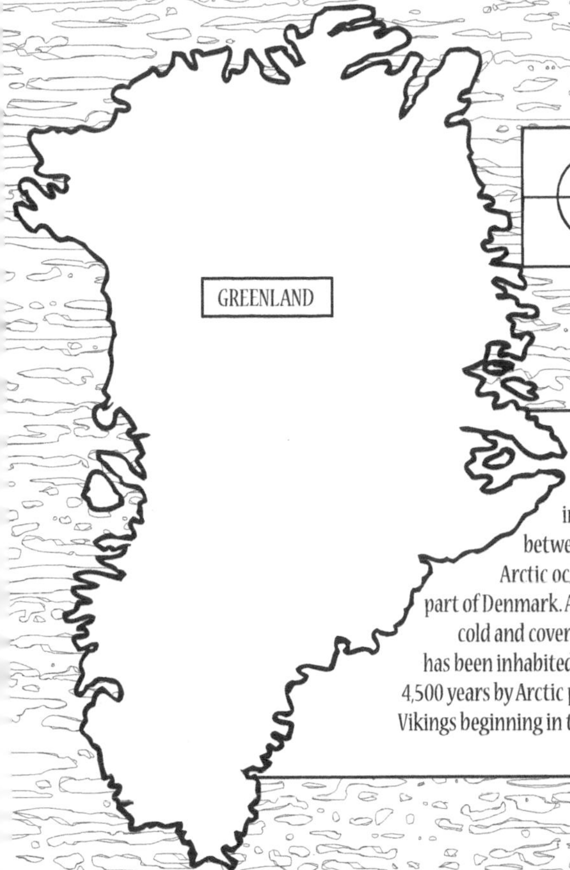

GREENLAND

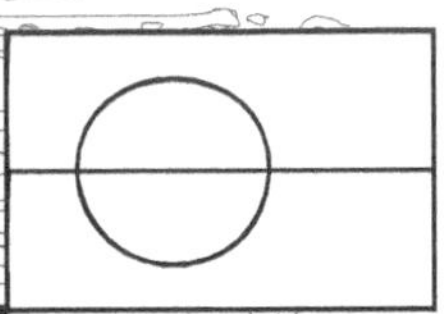

Greenland is the largest island in the world, nestled between the Atlantic and Arctic oceans and is actually part of Denmark. Although extremely cold and covered in ice, Greenland has been inhabited for at least the last 4,500 years by Arctic peoples and even by Vikings beginning in the 10th century AD.

The remote islands scattered across the Atlantic are almost all a part of 3 European countries: England, Spain, and Portugal. They were important stops for ships sailing back and forth from the New World across a turbulent and unpredictable ocean.

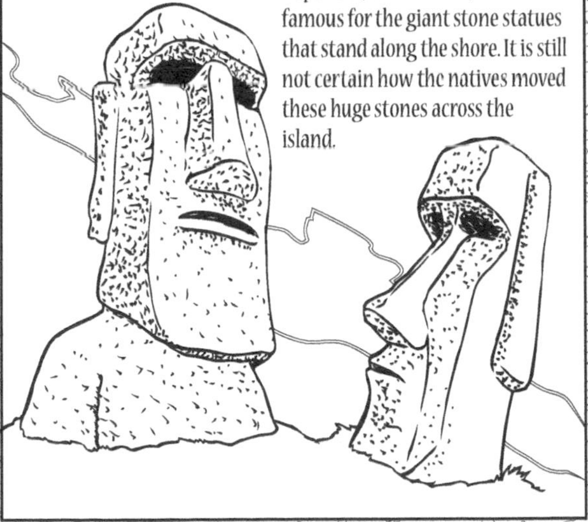

Rapa Nui (Easter Island) is world famous for the giant stone statues that stand along the shore. It is still not certain how the natives moved these huge stones across the island.

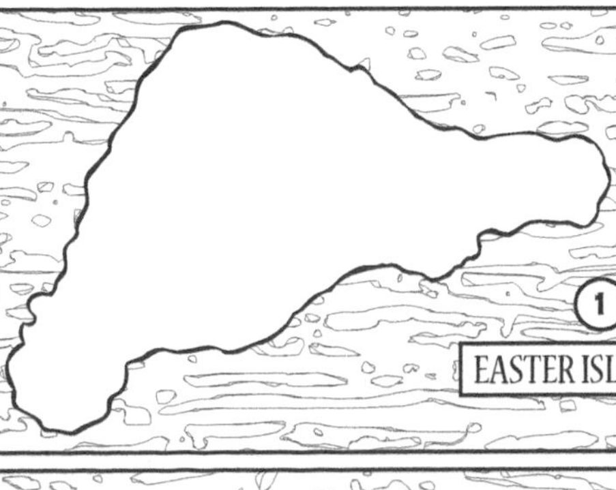

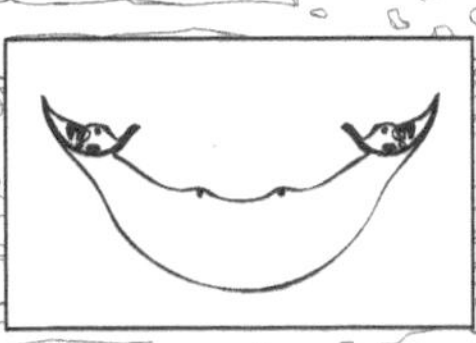

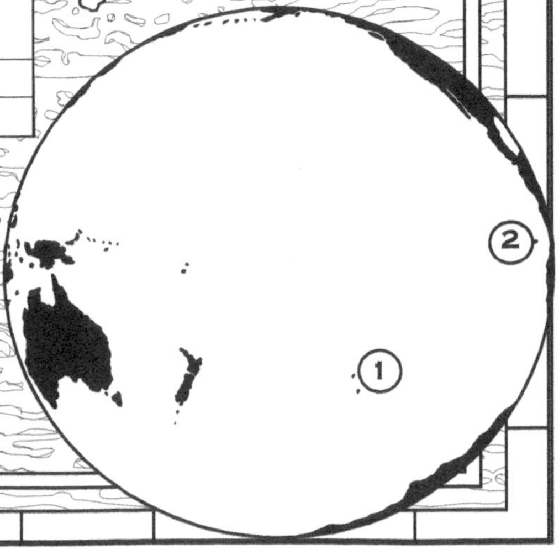

The marine iguana is found only on the Galápagos Islands and has the unique ability to live and hunt for food in the sea. It can dive over 30 ft into the water.

GALÁPAGOS ISLANDS

EASTER ISLAND (RAPA NUI)

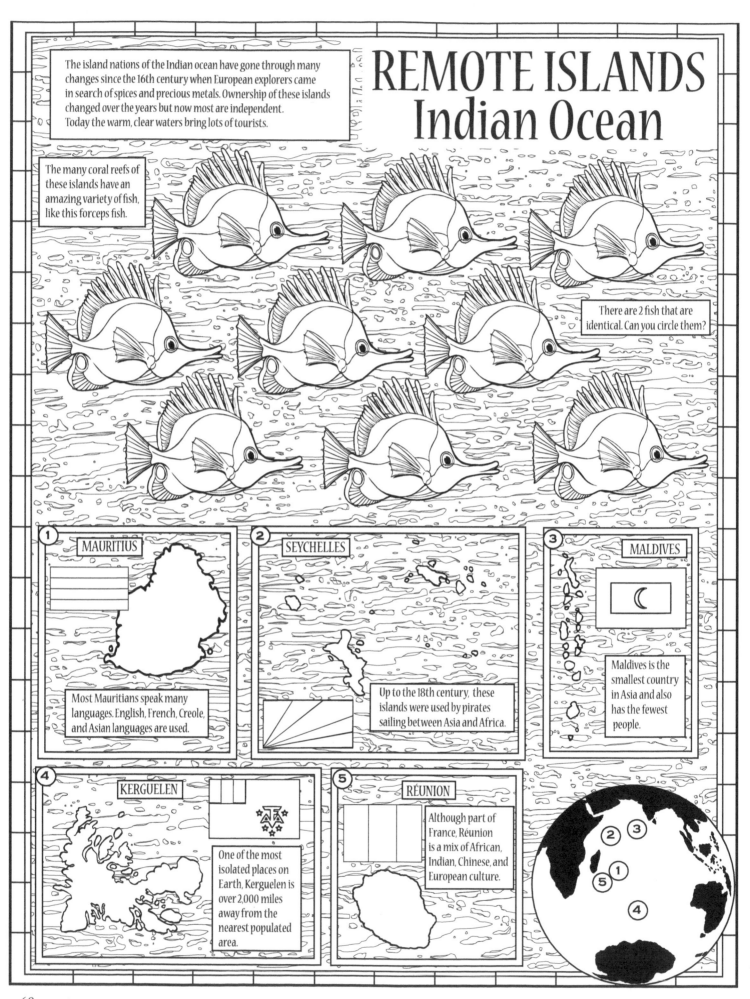

The island nations of the Indian ocean have gone through many changes since the 16th century when European explorers came in search of spices and precious metals. Ownership of these islands changed over the years but now most are independent. Today the warm, clear waters bring lots of tourists.

REMOTE ISLANDS
Indian Ocean

The many coral reefs of these islands have an amazing variety of fish, like this forceps fish.

There are 2 fish that are identical. Can you circle them?

① MAURITIUS

Most Mauritians speak many languages. English, French, Creole, and Asian languages are used.

② SEYCHELLES

Up to the 18th century, these islands were used by pirates sailing between Asia and Africa.

③ MALDIVES

Maldives is the smallest country in Asia and also has the fewest people.

④ KERGUELEN

One of the most isolated places on Earth, Kerguelen is over 2,000 miles away from the nearest populated area.

⑤ RÉUNION

Although part of France, Réunion is a mix of African, Indian, Chinese, and European culture.

PUZZLE SOLUTIONS

PAGE 4

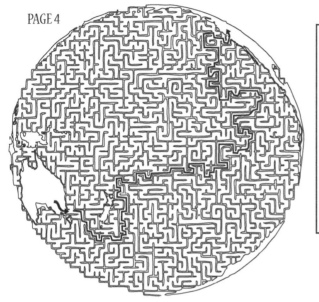

PAGE 6

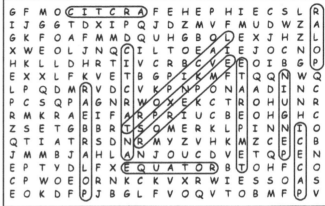

PAGE 9

HEMISPHERE crossword solution:
- 1. HEMISPHERE
- 2. MISSISSIPPI
- 3. TOMATOE
- 4. CORN
- 5. ALASKA
- 6. AMERICA
- 7. EASTERN
- 8. DISCOVERY
- 9. SAOPAULO
- 10. PACIFIC

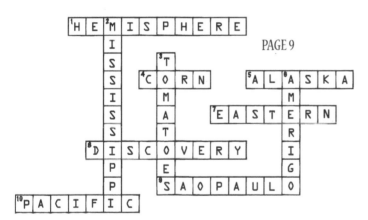

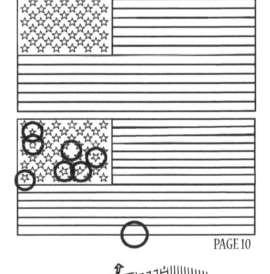

PAGE 10

PAGE 13

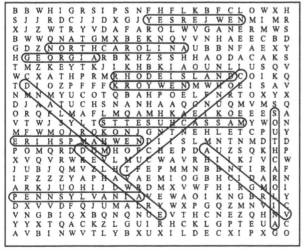

PAGE 15

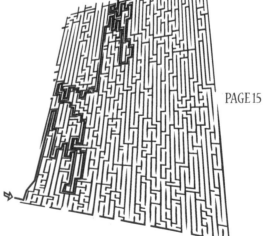

PUZZLE SOLUTIONS

PAGE 17

PAGE 19

YU**C**ATAN
ZAPOTEC
VAQUERO
GUADALAJARA
SONORA
PYR**A**MID
COPPER
GOVERNMEN**T**
EUROP**E**ANS
SAGUARO

AZTEC

PAGE 20

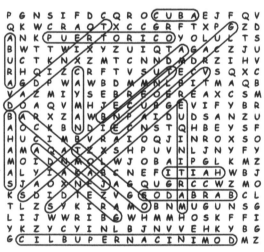

```
P G N S I F D C Q R O C U B A E J F Q V
Q K W C R A O T X C C G R F T X P G Z D
A N K P U E R T O R I C O Y O L U L T S
B U R A W T T W I X Y Z U I Q T A G A C Z I H V
U C H G R Q I Z C C R F T V S U E C V S Q X C
A G D P W A W B D M M N L P I T M A Q B
V A Z M I Y S E B R E O R E A X C M
D O A Q V M H T E C U R G E V I F Y B R
B A R X Z M W B N P A I D U D S A N Z U
A H A H B K N D I E N S T Q H B E Y S F
H U M O A G A T E X S H P U V N L J N Y F Y
A A O L I D N M O L W J O B A I P G L M Z
M A L Y I A E A B C N E F I T I A H W B J
A S A O X N P J A G Q U G R C C W Z M O
S K S D I D T E Z V G S O D A B R A B G L
T L Z S Y K I R A M O B N M U G U N S G
L I J W W R I B G W H M M H O S K F F I
U K Z Y C Y I N L B J N V V E H K Y B G
G C I L B U P E R N A C I N I M O D M Z
```

PAGE 22

PAGE 26

```
I S K A E M A N W Q M O R R Y W S I C J
P T E C W G U P M M E I O M T H K A U H I
L B O L E D S A O P A U L O O I P Q Z C
V O G K X P N B W E S X P L P W D E Y H C B C
E X E O B R K S N P W X U D K Z J A Y Q I O K B E N
X P G B B J B O O Q F X B Z J A U R C E C L
O Q Y H S F O Z P E H M B I T O O X R N
U A V M V V J C Z E D W A F O F V R K M
K O B C L E C G N E C C I K A R D E O R M N
H O Y B X A U Z E N B O T I P L N D R H
Y X I L M F N C V K P J R A M R L G U H
D C D I S I C E O T K K A O B L E I H U M
K K L S F N N E W N L E O B C N R C W L P L
P E J K C X W E W N L E D M D I X I I B
A T R J Z M Y U E L S W N C R C Y Y L L B O
C F G E O R G E T O W N B O I B
B B R A S I L I A T L D L L Y X E B
O A Y T Z J V V S E M U O D O V C J L E I C
D U B L L D V K R R J H Q J W G A F E R
D J G V I Z T G K V J S O C A R A C A S
```

PAGE 25

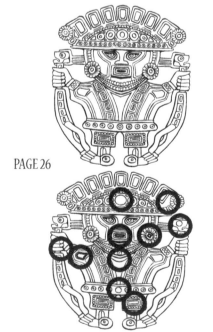

PAGE 62

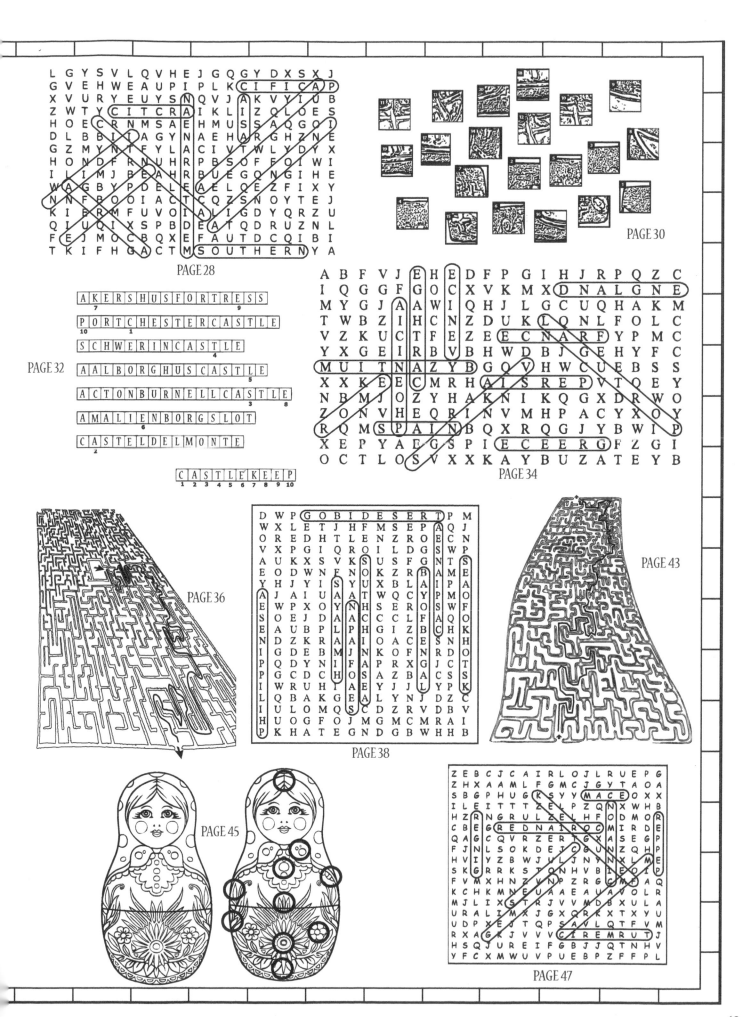

PAGE 28

PAGE 30

PAGE 32

PAGE 34

PAGE 36

PAGE 38

PAGE 43

PAGE 45

PAGE 47

PUZZLE SOLUTIONS

PAGE 48

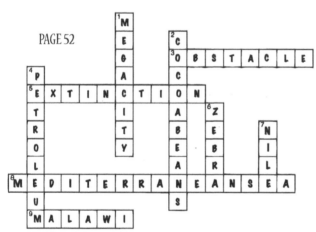

PAGE 51

S	O	U	T	H	E	R	N	O	C	E	A	N

M	A	R	Q	U	E	S	A	S	I	S	L	A	N	D	S

F	R	E	N	C	H	P	O	L	Y	N	E	S	I	A

N	O	R	F	O	L	K	I	S	L	A	N	D

M	A	R	S	H	A	L	L	I	S	L	A	N	D	S

S	O	L	O	M	O	N	I	S	L	A	N	D	S

N	E	W	C	A	L	E	D	O	N	I	A

P	A	R	A	D	I	S	E
1	2	3	4	5	6	7	8

PAGE 52

Across and down crossword solution:

1. MEGACITY
2. COCABEANS
3. OBSTACLE
4. PETROLEUM
5. EXTINCTION
6. ZEBRA
7. NIL
8. MEDITERRANEANSEA
9. MALAWI

PAGE 55

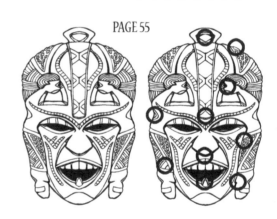

PAGE 57

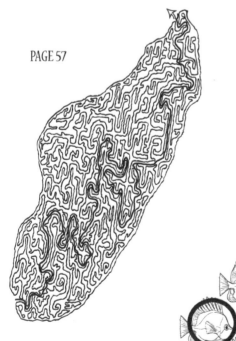

PAGE 58

D	S	H	C	A	N	A	R	Y	I	S	L	A	N	D	S	A	A	A	W
D	S	D	B	L	O	G	G	J	M	U	C	Y	O	E	D	H	S	L	S
C	M	A	N	C	S	L	Q	L	N	S	B	W	Q	S	J	N	C	G	V
L	R	D	I	A	B	F	C	X	V	A	R	H	K	G	K	U	E	F	R
M	N	R	E	N	L	S	D	D	Z	M	R	B	A	O	O	C	N	W	K
E	V	G	C	X	T	S	I	N	A	X	A	Y	N	B	D	A	S	R	E
G	I	I	B	K	V	H	I	D	H	B	A	F	R	Q	K	D	I	Z	Z
S	D	N	A	L	S	I	E	D	R	E	V	E	P	A	C	N	O	B	H
C	M	K	A	A	S	I	W	L	N	S	E	R	O	Z	A	A	N	M	H
H	H	T	X	D	R	X	V	I	E	A	Q	H	I	C	H	T	T	A	C
N	T	A	G	A	V	T	Q	Z	A	N	L	C	G	M	U	S	K	P	V
R	B	D	B	X	X	U	P	B	K	W	A	K	U	G	S	I	K	B	H
J	J	P	O	Z	O	I	M	D	O	Z	Y	Y	L	V	K	R	G	H	E
L	E	S	O	O	G	L	Y	E	J	N	O	X	Q	A	O	T	I	J	J
G	N	X	O	Q	W	V	I	C	N	U	T	D	U	K	F	B	X	N	D

PAGE 60

64